Alexander Balmain Bruce

The chief end of revelation

Alexander Balmain Bruce

The chief end of revelation

ISBN/EAN: 9783337414061

Printed in Europe, USA, Canada, Australia, Japan

Cover: Foto ©Lupo / pixelio.de

More available books at **www.hansebooks.com**

BY

ALEXANDER BALMAIN BRUCE, D.D.,

Professor of Apologetics and New Testament Exegesis, Free Church College,
Glasgow; Author of "The Training of the Twelve," "The Humiliation
of Christ," Etc.

NEW YORK.

ANSON D. F. RANDOLPH & COMPANY,

900 BROADWAY, COR 20th STREET.

PREFACE.

Portions of the contents of this volume were recently delivered as Lectures at the Presbyterian College, London. I have taken occasion from the opportunity thus afforded, to write at greater length, and with more fulness, than was necessary for the immediate purpose, on a subject which appears to me of great importance in its bearing both on Christian Apologetics and on the internal life and future fortunes of the Church. Two convictions have been ruling motives in this study. One is, that in many respects the old lines of apologetic argument no longer suffice either to express the thoughts of faith or to meet successfully the assaults of unbelief. The other is, that the Church is not likely again to wield the influence which of right belongs to her as custodian of the precious treasure of Christian truth, unless she show herself possessed of vitality sufficient to originate a new development in all directions, and among others in Doctrine ; refusing to accept as her final position either the agnosticism of modern culture, or blind adherence to traditional dogmatism. The last chapter of the book refers more particularly to this latter topic. The views there expressed may

satisfy neither liberals nor conservatives in theology.
I do not deprecate criticism, but I ask the critics to
remember that the apologist's task in these days is a
delicate one.   It will be observed that very frequent
reference is made to the author of the well-known
work, " Literature and Dogma." This was due to
one who is the accepted exponent of a wide-spread
tendency of thought on the subject of religion, whose
significance it vitally concerns the Church of the
present to understand.

THE AUTHOR.

GLASGOW, *April*, 1881.

TABLE OF CONTENTS.

CHAPTER I.

MISCONCEPTIONS.

CHAPTER II.

THE CHIEF DESIGN OF REVELATION.

CHAPTER V.

THE FUNCTION OF PROPHECY IN REVELATION.

CHAPTER VI.

THE DOCTRINAL SIGNIFICANCE OF REVELATION.

ERRATA.

Page 51, line 1, *for* raison d'être of its own existence, *read* reason of its own
    existence.
" 57, " 6, *for* that it is, *read* that is.
" 70, " 7, *for* the exclusion, *read* its exclusion.
" 73, " 5, *for* on those, *read* of those. Line 6, *for* of those, *read* on those.
" 108, " 20, *for* by the latter, *read* by them.

MISCONCEPTIONS.

CHAPTER I.

MISCONCEPTIONS.

My purpose in this book is to endeavour to form as definite ideas as possible concerning the chief design of revelation, or God's end in making that special manifestation of Himself above the plane of nature, whereof the Bible is the literary record—and to bring the ideas thus formed to bear on past and present controversies, as aids to faith and barriers against unbelief. On first view this may appear a very superfluous task. Who, it may be asked, does not know the answer to the question, What do the Scriptures principally teach? Yet nothing is more certain than that vague or erroneous notions have been and still are entertained on this subject both by believers and by unbelievers; creating unnecessary perplexities, giving rise to false inferences and objections, affording opportunities of attack, and occasions for defence, which disappear when the true state of the case is understood. The answer of the Westminster Assembly's Shorter Catechism, to the question above propounded, may itself be cited as an instance in point. "The Scriptures principally teach," we are told, "what man is to believe concerning God, and what duty God requires of man." The statement is too vague and general, and is thus fitted to become the cause, if it be not it-

self the effect, of misconception.   But the crude notions I have in view are not mere relics of a bygone
time ; we meet with them in current literature, in such
popular books, *e.g.*, as Mr. Matthew Arnold's "Literature and Dogma," and Mr. W. Rathbone Greg's
"Creed of Christendom."   In these books attacks are
made on the faith, which are based on certain assumptions as to the *raison d'être* of revelation, and the only
effectual method of meeting the assault is to form
exact ideas on the subject to which these assumptions
relate.   When it is considered how vital the questions
involved in the controversy are, it will at once be seen
how very incumbent on the apologist it is to undertake that task.   They relate to such cardinal topics
as the *possibility and verifiableness* of revelation ; the
function of *miracle* and *prophecy* in connection with a
revelation ; the *method* of revelation, involving advance
from rudeness to perfection along a regular course of
development, the employment of morally defective
agents, and the adoption of the principle of election,
that is, the principle of first bestowing privilege on
the few in order to the eventual communication of
the benefit to the many ; and, to specify only one
other point, the *doctrinal significance* of revelation.
Though the Bible is not directly, or in the first rank,
involved in this discussion (for Revelation must not
be confounded with its literary record, or the term
used as a synonym for the Scriptures—of this more
hereafter), yet it too suffers from misconceptions on
the fundamental question, What was God's chief end
in making a supernatural manifestation of Himself in
the sphere of human history?

  In view of the momentous issues involved, the utility

of a careful consideration of the class of topics which
cluster around the question will, I venture to think,
be generally conceded. This conviction will support
me in the endeavour to execute the task which I have
taken in hand, not without diffidence and a grave
sense of responsibility. What I aim at is not ency-
clopædic completeness, but to suggest some service-
able thoughts on the most pressing matters. To
achieve even this modest piece of work in a slight and
sketchy manner will require six lengthy chapters. I
devote this first introductory one to a statement of
the principal misconceptions which have been or still
are entertained on the subject of our study.

These misconceptions, then, fall into two general
classes. First, there are those which take a theoretical or doctrinaire view of revelation, and next, there
are those which go to the opposite extreme and take
an exclusively practical or ethical view of the same
subject. This classification does not resolve itself into
a distinction between the views of believers and those
of unbelievers respectively; on the contrary, believers
and unbelievers or freethinkers may be found on the
same side. Especially does this hold good, as we
shall see immediately, in reference to the doctrinaire
class of ideas.

Common to all patrons of theoretical or doctrinaire
conceptions are these two opinions; that *Revelation*
is to be identified with the *Bible*, and that the Bible
was given by God to men for the purpose of communicating doctrinal instruction on certain topics of
importance. This may be said to be the old view
held in common both by believer and by infidel. The
points on which those who adopted this view differed,

had reference to the subjects on which instruction was supposed to be given, and, as connected with that, the extent and character of the information vouchsafed. The sober, intermediate, what we may call the orthodox, opinion was that the knowledge communicated in the Scriptures relates to God and to human duty and destiny, and that it contains numerous items of information which could have been obtained from no other source. From this medium position some diverged by excess, others by defect. The excess consisted in looking on the Bible as a book containing miscellaneous information, of a more or less curious character, on all sorts of subjects ; not merely on God, duty, the future life, and such moral and religious topics, but on the secrets of nature, the problems of philosophy, the constitution of the heavenly world, etc. The extreme instance of this unlimited construction of the term Revelation is to be found in the Jewish *Kabbala*, which, by an arbitrary and grotesque system of interpretation, converted the Old Testament into a book of science, philosophy, and magic, as well as a book of moral law and religion. Milder examples of the *Kabbalistic* treatment of Scripture (using the epithet with reference, not to the *method* of interpretation, but to the character of the results obtained) have been supplied in more recent times by those who have been of opinion that the sacred Book, though not meant principally to teach the science of nature, yet contains latent in its pages important scientific hints, and always expresses itself in reference to natural phenomena with scientific accuracy. The conflicts in which this view has involved believers in Revelation and science in its onward progress are so familiar to all that it is not necessary to speak of them particularly. Suffice it to say, that these collisions have gradually taught faith the necessity of caution in the claims which she advances in behalf of the Bible, and led to the general adoption of the position that the revelation contained in the holy Book relates to distinctively moral and religious truth, that it is not intended to make known the secrets of the universe, and that when these Divine writings have occasion to speak of natural phenomena they do so, not in scientific, but in popular language. The old Kabbalistic idea, however, is not yet quite extinct; it lingers still, for venerable error dies hard; one meets with it now and then in odd corners of literature, and it may serve the purpose of a fresh illustration of a trite theme, and suffice as comment on the most obvious and gross abuse of the Bible, as a supposed repository of scientific lore, if I briefly allude to the latest instance which has come under my observation. I find it in a book with which I became acquainted during a late visit to America, entitled " Life : its true Genesis." * In respect of ability and knowledge the book is by no means to be despised ; on the contrary, its author shows himself to be well acquainted with the most recent scientific investigations, hypotheses, and discoveries, and discusses these with much acuteness, vigour, and spirit, which make the volume altogether enjoyable and exhilarating reading. But the writer is a dissenter from the views current in scientific circles on the origin of life, as taught by Darwin and

---

* By Mr. R. W. Wright. Published by G. P. Putnam's Sons, New York, 1880.

others. Dissatisfied with prevalent hypotheses and theories, he propounds one of his own which he endeavours to support by an induction of relative facts. The facts are interesting, and demand explanation on some theory. They are such as this, that when a forest consisting of a particular kind of tree, say pine, is cut down, it is succeeded by a growth, not of pine, but of oak, and that again by beech. The author believes such facts to be inexplicable on any current views of the origin of life, and he propounds his own theory to account for them, which is, that in the earth there are vital germs (not ordinary seeds) of all plants, and that whenever the necessary conditions come into existence, these germs manifest their presence in the bosom of the earth by sending forth a crop of vegetation. The germ differs from the seed in this, among other respects, in this above all, that a seed is always preceded by a plant, whereas the plant is always preceded by the vital germ. Now, as to this theory and the argument in its support, I am not going to call in question the facts alleged; they may be all true for aught I know to the contrary: neither do I quarrel with the theory; it may be as legitimate and as feasible as those it is meant to supplant. I certainly think neither the facts nor the theory should be treated with indifference or contempt; but, rather, carefully considered. The hypothesis is in some respects very plausible to say the least, as, *e.g.*, when it deals with the question of plant distribution. The "tramp" theory of distribution, according to which each plant had originally one native place on the earth's surface, whence individuals migrated in course of ages, is beset with serious difficulties, which the author of the "True

Genesis of Life" very acutely exposes. How simple and how tempting, in presence of these difficulties, the hypothesis that all the word over, the earth is filled with vital germs which develop into plants wherever the requisite conditions of soil, temperature, and the like prevail. Let the theory, therefore, receive, at the hands of competent judges, fair and full consideration. What I wish to point out is, that the author finds in Scripture support for his theory, on which he seems to rely more confidently than on all the facts of observation adduced. The Scriptural basis is discovered in a few Hebrew words in the first chapter of Genesis, rendered in our English version, "whose seed is in itself upon the earth," but which we are told ought to be rendered "whose germinal principle of life, each in itself after its kind, is upon the earth." That is to say, we are to understand that the Hebrew word *zera* is used by the sacred writer to express the scientific conception of a germinal principle existing in the earth antecedent to all plant life, created there by the energy of the Divine Spirit, not the popular idea of seed produced first by plants, and from which in turn plants are made to grow by the fertilizing influence of the soil. Is this probable? Even if the theory were established I should gravely doubt it, and still incline to hold, that in the text referred to, we are to find no anticipation of the new theory advanced by Mr. Wright, but a reference to the familiar fact that plants spring from seeds deposited in the ground. And on the other hand, should the theory on examination turn out a mistake, the authority of the sacred Book will not be compromised, because a sober exegesis will adhere to the principle, which painful experience

has taught the Church to respect, that on the phenomena of nature Scripture uniformly speaks not in
scientific or philosophic, but in popular language.
This principle may be held fast without prejudice to
the negative scientific merits of the Bible, such as the
invariable accuracy of its descriptive references to
natural phenomena, and the still more important fact
of its steering clear of all false science, especially from
any theological and superstitious views of nature, such
as were current in the ancient world ; a feature which
comes conspicuously out in the Scripture account of
creation, compared, *e.g.*, with the Chaldean Genesis,
a feature, I may add, so remarkable that even freethinkers have been struck with it, though unwilling
to recognise therein, with believers, the sure trace of
a Divine guidance helping the sacred writer to avoid
Pagan error, and in all his representations to walk in
the light of a pure ethical monotheism.

In comparison with those who would treat the Bible
as if it were a repository of miscellaneous information
on all conceivable subjects, the dogmatist proceeds
rationally who uses it as a theological text-book given
for the express purpose of conveying doctrinal instruction on religious and moral themes, which it is
his business to draw out into distinct propositions,
and set forth in systematic order. He has the merit,
at least, of recognising that the proper sphere of Biblical teaching is to be found in morals and religion.
But even in his conception there is something out of
accordance with the actual fact, and unwholesome in
tendency. In making this statement I am not to be
understood as denying the competency or utility of
systematic theology. I not only admit, but strenu-

ously maintain, that revelation has a doctrinal significance; and I can imagine attempts at exhibiting such
significance in a systematic way, which should keep
the chief end of revelation steadily in view, and make
the whole system of doctrine revolve round it as a
centre, and assign to each individual truth its place of
importance in accordance with the nearness or remote-
ness of its relations to the centre. Such attempts, indeed, have been made, especially in recent times, and
might be referred to if needful. All I mean to say is,
that there are certain sins which easily beset one who
makes revelation consist in the suggestion by the Divine Spirit, to the minds of apostles and prophets,
conceptions of ideas and words concerning the dogmas of faith and the rules of conduct.* In the first
place, the habit of using the Bible as a quarry of proof-
texts for an elaborate system of doctrine, is apt to
render the mind insensible to all Biblical material that
cannot be utilised in that way. The amount of such
matter is not small. There is much that is beautiful
and valuable in the sacred writings which cannot be
manufactured into dogma, and possesses chiefly literary or devotional interest. It is to this fact Mr.
Arnold points in the title which he has given to his
well-known work on the Bible, " Literature and Dogma." Then, even that which can be utilised for dogmatic purposes, is likely, in the hands of the dogmatic
theologian, to lose its living characteristics, and be-

---

* In these very terms is Revelation described by Hollaz, a Lu-
theran divine, who flourished in the 17th century. His words are:
"Spiritus Sanctus Prophetis et Apostolis conceptus rerum et ver-
borum de dogmatibus et moribus suggessit." Quoted by Rothe, in
' Zur Dogmatik," p. 55.

come transformed into a dead thing. The Bible is a
rich wide tract of country, wherein the plants and
flowers of Divine truth grow in endless profusion and
picturesque variety. What we find in theological
systems based on Scripture texts is a *Hortus Siccus*,
or collection of dried plants, arranged according to
their specific resemblances for the purposes of science,
but with the life pressed out of them.

Further, the dogmatic mind, as we now conceive of
it, has no notion of progress in revelation. All Scripture given by inspiration is profitable for doctrine.
All texts or books of Scripture are alike good for
the purpose, without distinction of date. The earliest
books are as available as the latest. It is implied in
the dogmatic conception of revelation, that salvation
depends on the knowledge of certain doctrines. That
being so, the most ancient men of God must be
assumed to have been in possession of the requisite
saving knowledge, and traces of such knowledge may
therefore be looked for even in the oldest parts of
the Bible. The patriarchs needed the sum of saving
knowledge, therefore they had it, therefore it may be
found even in the book of Genesis. How untrue this
idea of the Bible, according to which the first book is
as good as the last, progress, growth, development is
ignored, and Christ is in the Old Testament and in all
its parts not merely as a germ, but as a tree, does
not need to be pointed out. It is now generally understood that even in Revelation the law of progress by
development obtains, and it is owing to its full recognition of this truth that the modern science of Biblical, as distinct from dogmatic theology, has become
the fruitful study that it is.

Another vice of the dogmatic spirit remains to be mentioned, viz., the lack of all sense of *proportion*, or of the relative importance of the truths taught in Scripture. Every proposition capable of being substantiated by clear proof texts, is to be received as matter of religious faith. God gave the book to teach men certain doctrines, the number of these being limited only by the extent to which the process of manufacturing theological propositions with proof texts attached can be carried; and who am I that I should presume to determine which are fundamental and which of secondary moment? Under the influence of such notions, a dogmatic system, instead of being an organism of truth developed out of one great ruling thought, is apt to degenerate into a mere encyclopædia of theological opinions professing to be derived from Scripture, in which the least important dogma receives as much prominence as the most fundamental; so that the student, while in the act of learning many truths, is in danger of losing sight of the one great truth which sheds its benignant lustre on the sacred page; the truth, viz., that in the Scriptures we have the record of the manifestation of a gracious purpose evolving itself, in the course of ages, and finding its eventual fulfilment in Jesus Christ. In this way it may happen to the dogmatic student of a completed revelation, to repeat the experience of the Jew in studying the Old Testament. The Jew searched the Scriptures as one who verily believed that in them he should find eternal life; but his search was all but futile, his labour mostly lost, because he failed to discern God's chief end in making the revelation of Himself recorded in the Hebrew

2*

writings, imagining that it was to be found in the law-giving on Sinai; whereby it came to pass that the law eclipsed, to his eye, the purpose of grace running all through the long ages of preparation, and blinded his mind even to its sunlight-glory as it shone in the face of Christ. The melancholy failure of the people to whom were given the oracles of God to appreciate the design of the gift, supplies a most significant historical illustration of the serious consequences such shortcoming may entail. Let us not imagine it is a lesson which does not concern us.

The seventeenth century was the great Protestant dogmatic epoch, during which the conception of the Bible just animadverted on was everywhere dominant. In the eighteenth century, on the other hand, we meet on every side a spirit of reaction against theological dogmatism. The dogma-building spirit had done its work amidst much controversy, and with incredible toil it had created vast systems of divinity, embodied in huge tomes which it would take half a lifetime to read. And the task, when done, turned out to be a thankless one. The world seemed weary of theological controversy, and turned away from the learned tomes with apathy, almost with loathing. Deism, Illuminism, Aufkälrung succeeded to scholastic orthodoxy, and taught, to willing ears, that the vast structure of supernatural and unintelligible doctrines was really of no practical value, seeing the essence of religion consisted in a few simple truths which all could understand, and which commended themselves to every unsophisticated mind. But while the dogmas were given up, the dogmatic conception of Revelation was retained. That conception was a

legacy eighteenth-century free-thought inherited from
seventeenth-century orthodoxy, which shaped its way
of regarding the Bible, and which it even turned into
a weapon of assault against the faith in a Divinely
revealed religion. The deist, not less than the dogmatist, had a doctrinaire idea of revelation. He
could not think of any purpose God could have in
view in giving a revelation, other than to communicate instruction. The point on which he differed
from the dogmatist was the nature and amount of the
instruction communicated. Men under the influence
of the eighteenth-century *Zeitgeist*, whether believers
or unbelievers, were disposed to reduce the truths
which God could be supposed to teach men in a
special revelation to a very small number indeed to
three in fact, which may be called the *Deistic Trinity*.
These three were—that there is a God just and, above
all, beneficent; that moral obligations are to be
acknowledged and obeyed, or the infinite nature of
duty; and that man is destined to immortality. If
God gave a revelation to man, it must have been to
republish and enforce these fundamental truths of
natural religion; whatever more was found in any
pretended revelation was either false or of subordinate importance. Here was the opposite extreme to
Kabbalism; diverging from the *via media* of dogmatic orthodoxy on the side of defect, as far as the
Rabbinical idea of revelation diverged therefrom on
the side of excess. All three agreed that the Bible
was a scholastic book; but the Kabbalist thought
it taught everything, the dogmatist confined its
teaching pretty much to theology, and the deist
was of opinion that it taught next to nothing, at

most only the few elementary truths of natural religion.

The most genial and friendly representative of the deistical tendency may be found in *Lessing*, the most cultured and influential apostle of German Illuminism. By the bent of his spirit, Lessing was a philosophic sceptic or free-thinker, but he did not assume an attitude of hostility or unbelief towards revealed religion. On the contrary, he professed to believe in Revelation, and set himself to discover its chief end and contents. He developed his views on these points in the well-known tract, entitled "The Education of the Human Race." God's aim in giving to the race the Bible, he held, was to educate it out of moral childhood and rudeness into manhood, and He sought to do this by communicating to men the knowledge of truths which reason could find out for itself, but not easily or soon. Education, in general, gives a man nothing which he could not have from himself, but it gives it sooner and easier. Even so revelation gives to man no truths which his reason would not eventually discover, but it gave and gives the most important of these truths earlier. The truths of chief moment which God taught the race in an order determined by the capacity of the pupil were—the *unity of God*, presented first in the form of belief in a national God, Jehovah; then, finally, in the form of a pure ethical monotheism learned by Israel from the wise Persians while in exile; the *sum of duty* set forth in the Decalogue, whose precepts were enforced by a promise of long life in the land of Canaan; and, finally, the *doctrine of immortality* communicated first to a select few in Old Testament times, and at length made the property of the million by Jesus Christ. In this process of moral and religious education the Old Testament served the purpose of a primer, and the New Testament was the second lesson-book, put into the child's hands when it had outgrown the first. Both were good in their place and time, but both are destined to be superseded when the child reaches manhood. Then comes in the everlasting gospel of reason, when men shall see without aid truths which, in earlier ages, God beneficently taught men by means of the sacred school-books; and when they shall have the law so written in the heart, that they will do the right without any hope of reward, whether temporal or eternal, as an inducement; when, nevertheless, though no longer needed as a motive to well doing, the faith in immortality shall be firmly rooted in the spirit.

The theory of Revelation now briefly sketched is very attractive, and not without some elements of truth. It supplies a credible motive for Divine action; for it is quite conceivable that God should communicate to men, by special revelation, truths of the moral reason which, in the course of ages, they could eventually discover, but not till much later than they actually become acquainted with them through Divine aid, in oder that their higher education might be thereby accelerated. Then the notion of education, though not exhausting the idea of revelation, does enter into it as an element. When God entered upon the process of self-manifestation, of which we have the literary monument in the Scriptures, He did take in hand the moral and religious education of mankind. Even the idea of the lesson-books being superseded when they have served their

purpose has a certain germ of truth in it. That idea
is borrowed, we may say, from the Apostle Paul, who
justified the abrogation of the Mosaic law by com-
paring it to the system of tutors and governors to
which the heir of an inheritance is subject only till
the time of his majority has arrived. Lessing was
mistaken only in assuming that the time might come
when Christianity itself, as taught in the New Testament, should be superseded by the religion of reason,
even as the Jewish religion was superseded by it;
whereas, according to the teaching of the New Testament, and in truth, Christianity is the perfect
religion; God's last, because His full, adequate, absolutely true word to men; which cannot be outgrown
in thought as the world advances in wisdom, any
more than the Son, by whom that last word was
spoken, can be outgrown in moral worth. But it is
important to note the source of his mistake. It lay
in this, that his idea of revelation was exclusively
pedagogic. The Bible consists of two lesson-books,
which the pupil outgrows one after the other, as
pupils outgrow all school-books. He learns his
lessons about the unity of God, the moral law, and
the life to come, and goes his way, and thinks no
more about the primer and the second book. But
suppose that revelation consisted in something much
higher than moral education, even in the manifestation of a redemptive purpose, in the exhibition to our
faith of God as the God of Grace, so supplying not
only knowledge of duty, but power to become sons
of God; and suppose that in the Bible we have the
record of such a manifestation and exhibition,—could
we then think of outgrowing the holy writings as

worn-out school-books? As well might we think of outgrowing the sun; for Christ is the Sun of our souls, because He is the Saviour of our souls, and no one who recognises in Him the Redeemer will ever dream of the possibility of His being superseded. Nor will the book which bears witness to His redeeming love ever lose its interest, or its value as an atmosphere through which the rays of the spiritual Sun are diffused abroad over the world. Only such as think of Christ as merely a Teacher, and of Christianity as a system of ideas, will imagine that they can now dispense with both Christ and the New Testament. Even they are mistaken in their fancy. They are not so independent as they think. Some Christian light may indeed remain in their minds after they have thrown Christ and the gospel aside; it is, however, but as the twilight which remains in the sky after the sun has gone down, destined soon to fade into darkness.*

* " If Christianity be the revealed, and in principle completed, religion of redemption, and therefore the completion of all religion, an advance of religion beyond Christianity, or a perfectibility, or completion of Christianity itself, is neither possible nor necessary; therefore attempts of this kind lead away from religion in order to set in its place philosophy and esthetic for the benefit of demigods, who no more, like us common men, need religion " (Alex. Schweitzer, " Die Christliche Glaubenslehre, vol. iii. p. 5). This writer, in the same volume, p. 31, says again : " If Christianity were not the religion of redemption itself, as living piety, but only the doctrine of the same, we could cherish for Christ essentially only such a feeling as we entertain towards other great Church teachers ; viz., thankfulness for instruction given at a certain time, and for the spirit with which it was communicated in spite of powerful opponents." These views are the more worthy of note that the author by no means occupies an orthodox standpoint.

If in Lessing we see one who, while a true child of an unbelieving time, still endeavoured to reconcile faith in a doctrinal revelation with the prevalent theological liberalism, we find in another man, whose name is closely associated with his, an example of a free-thinker, using orthodox conceptions of revelation to subvert the orthodox faith in revelation. I refer to Reimarus of Hamburg, author of an unpublished work entitled "A Defence of the Rational Worshippers of God," from which Lessing extracted the pieces which he gave to the world under the name of "The Wolfenbüttel Fragments." This man, to whom Lessing, and more recently Strauss, has given greater prominence than he deserves, claims our attention chiefly on account of the principles on which his attack on revealed religion is based. He commenced his inquiries into the claim of the Bible to be a Divine revelation, by laying down these two positions: (1) that if a revelation was to be made it would be given in the form of a system of doctrine expressed in precise terms; and, (2) that men of irreproachable lives would be selected to be the medium of communication. In the preface of his work, according to Strauss, who took the pains to prepare and publish a digest of its contents, he gives an account of the origin of his doubts concerning the truth of revealed religion. The first thing that caused him to stumble was the fact that the Bible is not a doctrinal compendium. If God were to favour mankind with supernatural instruction for their salvation, He would, without doubt, adopt the most convenient form of an orderly and clear exposition, in which all that pertained to a doctrine of faith, or a system of morals, was brought together and expressed in a definite manner, and not scattered here and there, or confusedly mixed, or left vague and darkly worded. We observe in this assumption an instructive illustration of the way in which men's minds may be biassed in religion by their philosophy. Like most members of the Illuminist fraternity, Reimarus was a *Wolfian* in philosophy, and an admirer of the demonstrative mathematical method of his master, and hence he was prejudiced against the Bible, because forsooth its Divine Author had not adopted the style of a philosopher belonging to the Wolfian school. Another thing which greatly scandalized the doubter, was the character of the people whom God chose to be the recipients of revelation, and of the so-called men of God whom He used as His instruments, or who figure prominently as worthies in the Scriptures. He could not conceive God choosing so stiff-necked, ignoble, and perverse a race to be a peculiar people in preference to other more teachable and gifted nations; and in the actions of the Bible characters—the patriarchs, Moses, Samuel, David, etc.—he found traits which made it impossible for him to regard them as men after God's heart, and messengers of His revelation.

It is easy to understand how one coming to the examination of the Bible with such assumptions in his mind could not fail to find in it many stumbling-blocks. For in truth the sacred Book is as far as possible from being a systematic compendium of religious instruction. No book in the world has less the appearance of bearing that character. It is most interesting, excellent, edifying " literature," but it is not a book of "dogma," whatever dogmas may be extracted from it by legitimate exegesis. So far are the recipients of revelation from being men whom God is using for conveying doctrinal instruction of a formal character to the world, that some of them seem to receive little teaching themselves, and to give none at all to others. The patriarchs for example: what do they learn from God, or what contribution do they make to the compendium of religious doctrine? Why the communications made to them refer, as Reimarus observed, to his amazement, not to abstract topics, such as the unity of God, or the immortality of the soul, but rather to such gross worldly matters as children and lands; and instead of going about as missionaries teaching the true religion, their whole concern seems to be about flocks and herds and wells, and marriages and offspring. Most perplexing behaviour, truly, on the part of men who are supposed to be God's agents in the work of communicating to the world a doctrinal revelation! But to infer therefrom that no Divine revelation has taken place, is somewhat precipitate. What if the proper inference were that the conception of revelation, cherished by Reimarus in common with the orthodox, from whom he received it by tradition, was an altogether mistaken one? What if the revelation consisted not so much in the communication of a body of truth, as in the intimation of a gracious purpose? In that case the prominence given to such matters as an heir, or a land, which seems so utterly out of place in a doctrinaire revelation, may be found not altogether inexplicable. In a similar way, revision of the idea of revelation might go far to remove the scandals arising out of the lives of the

men of revelation. It certainly must be admitted
that they were far enough from being perfect men.
No need for a microscope to discover faults in most
of them ; no need for such elaborate efforts to convict
many of them of grievous shortcomings, as Reimarus
makes, till his reader is wearied, not to say disgusted.
The fact stares one in the face. But what then ; does
grievous faultiness disqualify men for being the agents
of Divine revelation? Must God in giving a revelation play the Pharisee, and out of a regard to His dignity have to do only with perfect characters? Or is
it due to the world that its teachers should be so very
far above the general level in virtue? There might
be something to be said for these positions if revelation consisted in communicating ideas of reason, ethical precepts, or maxims of wisdom. But what if the
revelation consist in a self-manifestation of God as the
God of grace? Then we shall not wonder at the Divine Being condescending to have intimate relations
with erring mortals, or making known His will for the
world's redemption, by men participating, more or less,
in the world's sin.

The employment of a doctrinaire conception of revelation as a weapon of assault against faith in a supernaturally revealed religion is a device not yet antiquated. We find this same conception used to assail
the possibility and the verifiableness of revelation by
so respectable and influential a writer as the author
of " The Creed of Christendom." In that work Mr.
Greg propounds for discussion the question : Is Christianity a revealed religion? and he thus defines the
position taken up by those who answer the question
in the affirmative : " When a Christian affirms Chris-

tianity to be a revealed religion, he intends simply
and without artifice to declare himself that the doctrines and precepts which Christ taught were not
the production of His own human mind, either in its
ordinary operations or in its flights of sublimest contemplation, but were directly and supernaturally communicated to Him from on high.   He means this, or
he means nothing definable or distinctive." This
state of the question he afterwards paraphrases thus:
" It remains therefore a simple question for our consideration whether the doctrines and precepts taught
by Jesus are so new, so profound, so perfect, so distinctive, so above and beyond parallel, that they could
not have emanated naturally from a clear, simple, un-
soiled, unwarped, powerful, meditative mind, living
four hundred years after Socrates and Plato ; brought
up among the pure Essenes ; nourished on the wisdom of Solomon, the piety of David, the poetry of
Isaiah ; elevated by the knowledge, and illuminated
by the love of the one true God."   These two extracts
clearly set forth the author's point of view.   Revelation consists in the supernatural communication of
truth which the human mind could not attain of itself,
and there is no reason to believe that Jesus could not,
in His position and with His training, arrive in a natural way at the thoughts embodied in His recorded
sayings ; in other words, no reason to regard Jesus
otherwise than as one of the world's wise men.   But
Mr. Greg goes further than this.   He not only holds
that as matter of fact no supernatural teaching was
necessary to give Jesus His wisdom, but strives to
prove that supernatural teaching in general is *impossible*, or at least unverifiable.   This he does by means

of the two following questions: Can the human mind receive an idea which it could not originate? and how can a man distinguish between an idea revealed to him and an idea conceived by him? The questions are rather loosely put. It is assumed, for instance, that an idea and a truth are the same thing. The author indeed affirms that they are. " A truth," he says, " is only an idea, or a combination of ideas, which approves itself to us." But a truth is something more than a combination of agreeable ideas. An illustration will best show this. God is one idea, love is another; the combination of these two ideas is agreeable to our hearts; but that is a very different thing from knowing it to be true, to be a real objective truth that God *is* love, as the Apostle John affirms. And this illustration may also help us to understand how we may be able, without Divine aid, to conceive and even to combine ideas, and yet may require such aid to regard the combination as objective truth. I do not need Divine revelation to give me the idea of God; as little do I need such help to give me the idea of love. I can also, without supernatural succour, combine these two ideas. I can *imagine* God being love. To do that is easy, but, alas, to believe that God is love is not so easy. After I have conceived such a thing as a possibility, I stand very much in need of assurance that my conception is not only a possibility, but a fact. Suppose now we translate Mr Greg's question into accurate language, and ask: Can the human mind receive a truth by revelation which it could not certainly know to be true otherwise, though it might be able to conceive of its possibility? Why not? Where is the difficulty? The puzzle disappears as soon as it is stated in proper terms. To convert possibilities, conceived but not firmly believed, into certainties, was one grand design of revelation. And now observe, with reference to Mr. Greg's second question, how this is done. Take again the infinitely momentous truth that God is love. How am I to be assured of that truth with a measure of assurance far surpassing that attainable by the light of nature, which confessedly leaves Divine love, to a large extent, problematical? How shall I know, *e.g.*, whether love means for God what it means among men, viz., a spirit which makes a man willing to sacrifice himself for another, as Alcestis sacrificed herself for her husband? I can conceive such a thing as possible. I cannot indeed think of God as love without the conception entering into my mind. But from the conception to the belief what a distance! Is it possible that God can or will sacrifice Himself, or stoop to be a burden-bearer to His own creatures? How shall I know, save by God doing the thing, and so showing me that love is the reality for Him that it is for all the moral heroes who sacrifice themselves for others? And the doing of it is the revelation. Christ's death on the cross is the most important part of His revelation; far more important than His words of wisdom, precious as these are. And the radical error of Mr. Greg is, that he takes account only of the latter, leaving out of view the revelation which Christ made in His life, in His actions, and, above all, in His passion. It is the old traditional error of a doctrinaire conception of revelation reproduced in our age, and made the basis of an ingenious attempt to demonstrate the impossibility of revelation, which is seen to be inept so soon as the

subject in debate is rightly defined. That Mr. Greg's
attack would be valid even against revelation as conceived by himself, I am not to be understood as admitting. All I mean now to point out is, that there
is a way of regarding revelation, with reference to
which his argument does not even possess plausibility.

In proceeding now to give some account of the
opinions of those who have taken a purely practical
or ethical view of the chief end of revelation, I must
go as far back as the seventeenth century to find the
first influential representative of this tendency in post-
reformation times. The man to whom must be assigned this important position is the famous Amster-
dam Jew, Benedict Spinoza, justly regarded as the
father of modern pantheism. Spinoza was not only
the first, but also the most thorough-going exponent
of the purely ethical conception of the aim of the
Bible, which is so much in favour with many at the
present time; and on this account, as well as out of
regard to his general position in the history of
modern speculative and theological thought, he is
entitled to very special attention. The fact of his
belonging to the seventeenth century, and to Holland,
readily suggests the conjecture that his peculiar way
of viewing revelation may have been due to reaction
against the dogmatic spirit of the age, which manifested itself with special intensity in that country in
connection with the disputes between the Calvinists
and the Arminians. Such, accordingly, we know
from Spinoza himself to have been the actual fact.
In the *Tractatus theologico-politicus,* the writing in
which his opinions on the present subject are set
forth, published anonymously in 1670, the author

clearly explains the occasion and design of his work.
In the preface he tells that he had observed, with
pain, the grievous evils of religious controversy, as
illustrated in all ecclesiastical history, and especially
in the recent dispute between the Arminians and
Calvinists (which led to the assembling of the Synod
of Dort): how in such disputes natural reason was
despised, and treated as the fountain of impiety, and
human opinions were taken for Divine truth, and
credulity deemed faith, and philosophical controversies keenly agitated in Church and State; whence
arose savage hatreds and dissensions, breeding sedition
and schism. Observing these melancholy phenomena,
it occurred to him to ask whether they did not all arise
out of an illegitimate use of Scripture, as an authority
in matters of philosophical and theological opinion in
which reason should be left to its liberty. Men were
fiercely wrangling about predestination and election,
the depravity of human nature, irresistible grace, and
the like topics. What if the Bible was never intended
to decide such questions; what if the opinions it contains bearing thereon be not even mutually consistent, and are to be taken simply for what they are
worth, as the personal opinions of the particular
writers speaking according to the best light they
possessed? With this idea in his mind he resolved,
he tells us, to examine Scripture anew with unbiassed
mind, and to affirm nothing concerning it, and admit
nothing as to its teaching, which was not in accordance with its ascertained character. His enquiry related to such topics as these: What was prophecy,
and how did God reveal Himself to the prophets, and
on what ground were they acceptable to God, whether

because of the truth or value of their thoughts of God
or of nature, or simply because of their piety; in
what sense were the Hebrews an elect people; whether
miracles, so-called, happened contrary to the order of
nature, and whether they teach the existence and
providence of God more certainly and clearly than
the things which happen in the course of nature, and
whose causes are known; whether there was anything
in Scripture to justify the vilification of the human
intellect as corrupt and blind, a question whose settlement depended on this other; whether the religious
or Divine law revealed by prophets and apostles was
different from that which the natural light of reason
teaches? On all these questions he arrived at conclusions radically diverse from those current in the
Church. The authority of the prophets, he found,
had weight only in those things which bear on life
and morals: their opinions no way concern us. These
Hebrew prophets, on an examination of their history
and writings, appeared to be men of singular virtue,
who cultivated piety with great devoutness, and
hence, in Bible language, were said to be filled with
the Spirit of God, and to be men of God, just as a
stately cedar is called a cedar of God. Their chief in-
tellectual gift was a lively imagination. They were
not endowed with better minds than other men, and
therefore it is an entire mistake to seek in their writings wisdom and the knowledge of natural and spiritual things. All that we can learn from them is what
bears on the fear of God or obedience; in reference
to all else for anything the prophets teach, we may
believe what we please. This is apparent when we
consider the grounds of prophetic certitude, which

3

were these three: a vivid imagination of the things
" revealed," a sign specially given for the prophet's
satisfaction, and, above all, a mind steadily inclined
to goodness. The certainty thence arising was only
subjective. The second condition, indeed, may seem
to carry with it objective certitude, but it does not,
because the signs vouchsafed were adapted to the
capacity and opinions of the particular prophet, so
that what would convince one might fail to convince
another. Even the "revelations" made to the
prophets, were adapted not only to the temperament,
the imagination, and the outward circumstances, but
even to the peculiar, and it might be erroneous,
opinions of the individual. That the prophets held
erroneous opinions, and did not agree in their
opinions, is apparent from the record. The conclusion which results from all the facts, is, that we
must not expect to find in the prophetic writings,
that is in the Hebrew Scriptures generally, philosophically accurate views concerning God, but merely
such as tend to promote piety and morality, the
prophets not being raised by their prophetic gift
above liability to ignorance and error in regard to
matters of speculation, which have no bearing on
charity and practice. The author thought himself
justified in drawing from the phenomena a similar
inference in reference to the New Testament writings.
The apostles wrote as doctors, not as prophets sup-
porting their statements on a Thus saith the Lord,
and they differed from each other in their views.
They are not to be blamed for mixing up religion
with speculation, for the gospel was new, and they
were obliged to gain for it access to men's minds by

accommodating themselves to contemporary thought. But we may now disregard Paul's philosophy and theology, and attend only to the few elementary truths in the teaching of which prophets, apostles, and Christ are all at one. These truths Spinoza pronounced to be neither more nor less than the doctrines of natural religion, which the much decried reason teaches us by its own light.

It does not need to be pointed out to what theory of revelation these free and frankly expressed opinions conduct. The substance and the design of revelation have respect merely to piety and obedience. The Bible was not intended to teach, and does not in fact teach, any definite doctrines concerning God, or man, or the world; but has for its sole object to promote the practice of godliness, justice, and charity. The writers of the Bible did not themselves all hold the same opinions, and therefore it is vain to seek from their writings one uniform system of dogmas. A man may make a very wise, good use of these writings, and be a true believer in the Scripture sense, and yet hold all manner of opinions, theistic or pantheistic, concerning God. Faith consists in cherishing such sentiments concerning God as are necessary to and involved in obedience. It requires, not true, but pious beliefs. To the catholic faith belong no dogmas concerning which there can be controversy amongst honest men; in particular, no such dogmas as those relating to predestination or election. It is idle to appeal to the Scriptures to decide the controversy concerning election. Election, in the Old Testament, simply means that God chose for Israel a particular spot of the earth wherein they might live in safety and comfort. The Hebrew people were elected simply to outward privilege, not to exceptional knowledge of God, or to be made in an exclusive sense a holy people. In the New Testament there is a deeper doctrine of election, taught especially in Paul's epistles. But then Paul speaks as a theological doctor, and we must take his doctrine for what it is worth.

One wonders that a man holding such views should continue to speak of a revelation, or to believe in it in any special, distinctive sense. Indeed, we know that with his speculative opinions Spinoza could not believe in a revelation, in the sense of a communication of truth to men by the living God with the intention of promoting their happiness. He was a Pantheist, and believed in no living God, in no God capable of cherishing intentions or performing special acts. But he does not say so plainly in the *Tractatus*, but keeps his philosophy in the background, and accommodates his language to theistic opinions that he may reason with Theists on their own terms. Yet his speculative bias is plain enough from many indications, and very specially from the views which he expresses on the subject of miracles. These are in brief as follows: A miracle, in the sense of an event contrary to nature, is impossible, the order of nature being fixed and immutable. The so-called miracles of Scripture, if real occurrences, were simply events whose natural causes are unknown. If from the nature of the case any recorded event could not possibly have had a natural cause; *e.g.*, the resurrection of a dead man, then the narrative must be held to be false, and probably added to the sacred writings by sacrilegious hands. From miracles, however conceived, whether as events contrary to nature, or as events due to natural but obscure, unknown causes, we can learn nothing, either as to the being, or the essence, or the character of God. They are simply prodigies or accidents without significance. We can know God only through the fixed course of nature, whose laws are the expression of His eternal will and decrees. Of course, on this view, the miraculous element in Scripture, so far from being the medium of a very special revelation, is no revelation at all. Nay, on such a view of the miraculous, the very word revelation, as applied to Scripture, is evacuated of meaning, and its use ought to be discontinued, as fitted to foster delusion. For a special revelation, made with a definite purpose, is essentially miraculous; and if miracle is to be discarded, words which imply miracle should be discarded also. In the work we have been speaking of, Spinoza did not choose to be thoroughly self-consistent. He preferred to occupy *pro tempore* the position of one who believed the Bible to be the word of God, given for a special purpose. But he found himself somewhat at a loss to tell what the precise end served was. He supposes some one to ask the question, What is the use of the Bible, seeing we cannot learn from it any definite doctrine concerning the nature and attributes of God, but only a few elementary truths of morality and religion, such as the light of reason can reveal to thoughtful minds? And he gives this somewhat enigmatical answer: "Since we cannot perceive by the light of nature that simple obedience is the way to salvation, and that revelation alone teaches us that that is accomplished by the singular grace of God, which we cannot attain by reason, hence it follows that Scripture has brought an exceedingly great consolation to mortals. For while all without exception can obey, there are comparatively very few who acquire the habit of virtue by the sole guidance of reason; and therefore, unless we had the testimony of Scripture, we might doubt concerning the salvation of almost all men." These sentences produce the impression that their author was puzzled to discover a presentable ground for the necessity of revelation. His real opinion, doubtless, was, that a revelation was unnecessary, as, on his philosophy, we know it is impossible.

In the century following that in which Spinoza lived, the same tendency to connect the idea of revelation exclusively with practice was favoured by the founder of the critical philosophy and his disciples. Kant and Fichte were specially conspicuous advocates of the doctrine that the proper subject of all revelation is *law.* The former restricted the sphere of revelation still further, by conceiving of the laws specially revealed as statutory or positive precepts, in contradistinction from moral laws. The communication of such positive precepts by special revelation he represented as made necessary by the weakness of human nature. Not otherwise can a kingdom of God, or a society of men associated together for ethical ends, come into actual being. Such a society is very needful to help individuals to fight with evil and to do good; and if all men earnestly bent on obeying the law written on the heart were to unite together for mutual aid in the culture of morality, they would constitute a kingdom of God, or Church. But unfortunately men have never been able to establish an ethical society on the basis of the dictates of pure practical reason. They have ever been hard to persuade that a good life is all that God demands of them; they have imagined that their duty to Him must consist in some special service which He requires of them. But we can learn what service God requires of us, how He would have us honour Him,—so far as this honour goes beyond our general moral obligation, only by an express declaration of His will. This declaration, when made, is a revelation, the contents of which consist in a body of positive precepts relating to religious ritual. The abstract possibility of such a revelation Kant did not deny; but to maintain its reality in any given case he regarded as foolhardy, or as probably an act of intentional usurpation on the part of one who wished to increase his influence and authority over the people. Belief in such a revelation comes early in a people's history, and is made possible by their moral rudeness, of which their wise men take advantage to deceive them for their good.*

Fichte, on the other hand, conceived of revelation as having for its proper sphere moral law. The design of all possible revelation, in his view, could only be to bring the claims of the moral law to bear with increased power upon the minds of men in a weak rude moral condition. In his first publication, entitled An Attempt at a Criticism of all Revelation, which had for its aim to apply the principles of the Kantian philosophy to the subject of revealed religion, Fichte defined the idea of revelation as the idea of an

* *Vide* " Religion innerhalb der Grenzen der blosen Vernunft," III. i. 5 ; also Zeller, " Geschichte der deutschen Philosophie," p. 500.

appearance produced by the Divine causality in the
world of sense, whereby God makes Himself known
as moral Legislator. Such an appearance he admitted
to be physically possible, and, when taking place for
the purpose of educating morally rude men capable
of being influenced only by what addressed itself
to their senses, not unworthy of God; for, though it
may seem to degrade God by making Him a pedagogue, yet in truth nothing is unworthy of God that
is not contrary to the moral law. The Divine Being
may humble Himself in the interests of morality; and
if it be found impossible in any other way to promote
the moral education of the race than by a promulga-
tion of duty amid miraculous accompaniments fitted
to awaken awe, right reason cannot object to Deity
condescending to man's need. This theory seems to
have the merit of making room for at least such a
revelation of law as that made to Israel on Sinai.
The practical conclusion, however, of Fichte's criticism is a sceptical one. While the abstract possibility
of a revelation is admitted, its *verifiableness* is in
effect denied. Revelation, in Fichte's philosophy, as
in Kant's, comes to mean *belief* in revelation; and
the belief has its origin, not in any objective Divine
manifestation, but in devices of wise men to make an
impression on the minds of the multitude. It is the
old story of deceit for a beneficent purpose.*

Coming down, now, to our own time, we find the
ethical view of revelation, so called, espoused and
advocated with literary grace and persuasiveness by
Mr. Matthew Arnold in the work already referred to.
Mr. Arnold's way of regarding the Bible has more

* *Vide* Fichte's Werke, 5ter Band, p. 81.

affinity with Spinoza's than with that of the critical philosophers, in so far as it insists on the general tendency of the Scriptures to promote the habit of virtue, rather than on any special instruction which they convey on the rules of conduct. Of Spinoza Mr. Arnold remarks, that he is coming more and more to the front. The observation is just ; many things confirm it : the appearance of new editions of his works, of translations in our language of some of his particular treatises, such as the "Tractatus," of which I have already given some account, and of original studies in his life and philosophy ;* the increasing prevalence of Pantheistic modes of thought more or less traceable to his influence ; the prominent notice taken of his opinions on miracles and other topics in Apologetic literature. In one sense, the more he comes to the front the better, for to know Spinoza is the best way to understand modern philosophy and theology. In his "Ethics" we find a key which opens to us many mysteries in such writers as Hegel, Schelling, and Schleiermacher, I may indeed almost say in Continental systems of speculative thought generally. In that work is set forth in short compass, and in clear incisive style, and without reserve, the doctrines whereof more recent systems are to a large extent but voluminous and not very intelligible elaborations. In Spinoza we are at the sources of the Nile, starting from which we may with tolerable certainty track the

---

* The most recent work on Spinoza's life and philosophy, is that by Pollock, published in 1880. In the last chapter of this work the author gives an account of the influence of Spinoza on modern thought.

3*

downward course of the mystic river of Pantheism.
And if one wishes to know the practical outcome of
Pantheism, he need not leave the fountain head. As
from Spinoza he can learn the essential features of
the Pantheistic theory of the universe, so from him
also he can learn the weak points of the theory. For
in him is no disguise, no prudential reservation, no
accommodation to existing fashions of thought, on
such topics as human freedom, the reality of moral
evil, and the life to come; but a blunt denial of all
our most cherished beliefs on these and kindred topics.
But what I wished to say was, that no better evidence
of the truth of Mr. Arnold's remark concerning
Spinoza need be sought than that furnished in his
own writings. In "Literature and Dogma," in particular, Spinoza does come to the front dressed up in
attractive modern guise, as a smart modern man of
letters and child of nineteenth-century culture, but
still plainly recognisable by his unmistakable Jewish
physiognomy. "Literature and Dogma" is to a large
extent just the *Tractatus* popularized and reproduced
with much expository skill and easy grace of style.
Arnold, like Spinoza, conceives of the Bible as a book,
not of Dogma, but of Conduct. Its function is, not to
teach us doctrines about God or other transcendental
topics, but to set forth the supreme value of right
conduct; and its claim to the lasting reverence and
gratitude of mankind rests on the fact that it has
performed this high task incomparably well. So far
from being a book of dogmatic divinity, the Bible
does not so much as declare in a dogmatic theological
sense that God exists, or that He is personal, or that
He is a Being to whom you can with propriety apply

the masculine pronoun. But there is one thing the Bible does, over and above emphasizing the supreme importance of conduct. It recognises and proclaims with due emphasis the great truth that there is *a power in the world not ourselves making for righteousness*, tending to bring about a correspondence between character and lot, and so to make the good happy and the wicked miserable. This is not a dogma, but a fact which is capable of being verified by observation and by the study of history, and which may be admitted by all men, irrespective of their speculative opinions, by Atheists and Pantheists and Materialists, not less than by Theists. In this affirmation Mr. Arnold is certainly right, for the fact in question has been acknowledged by men of all schools, and by some it has been asserted with even greater emphasis than by himself; by none in modern times with more power than by Thomas Carlyle. The author of "Literature and Dogma" has the merit of coining a new phrase to describe the old fact; but his phrase means just what other men have spoken of by other names. Even Strauss, Atheist and Materialist though he was in his later days, acknowledged the fact denoted by Mr. Arnold's *Power not ourselves*, under the name of the *moral order of the world*, in some respects a preferable expression. But the author of "Literature and Dogma" makes no claim to have discovered the fact. The service which he claims to have rendered in his work, is to have duly directed the attention of his contemporaries to the relation of the Bible writers to the fact, which he thinks has been greatly lost sight of in consequence of the misuse of the Bible by professional interpreters, who have looked into the sacred writings only for their pet dogmas. The Bible writers, he tells us, though they lived many centuries ago, had eyes to discern this great fact. They have also been able in their writings to give it adequate powerful expression. Properly speaking, these writings have no other aim than to assert the fact in every possible form, as a motive to right conduct. They do not all assert it in the same way. The Old Testament writers sought the proofs that the Power not ourselves is at work too much in outward lot; and inasmuch as that power in its working only *tends* to unite righteousness and felicity, and does not by any means fully reach the goal, their minds became perplexed, and they set about supplementing their grand fundamental doctrine by inventing fairy tales about a Messiah and a Messianic kingdom, and a life hereafter. Jesus came and taught men a new method of getting the reward of righteousness, which made them independent of outward events; the method, viz., of seeking felicity within, in the state of the spirit; and a new secret for bringing blessedness into the heart, viz., self-denial. His was the perfect doctrine. But even the ancient Hebrew prophets, with all their errors and superstitions, rendered an inestimable service to mankind by their proclamation of the truth that conduct is the supremely important thing and that the Power not ourselves,—what they called the Eternal God,—is on the side of righteousness. This doctrine was worthy to be called a revelation, if any utterances of the human mind may receive that name ; and the Bible is the best of all books because, more than all other books, it directs men's attention to that which is at least three-fourths of human life, and more to be regarded by far than culture, or art, or any other human interest. After we have removed from the ancient book all that is erroneous or worthless,— miraculous narratives, fairy tales of a future golden age, incredible dogmas,—there remains a large mass of inestimably precious material devoted to the praise of righteousness and the inculcation of pure moral-ity, with an enthusiasm which raises ethics to the dignity of religion.

I have no desire to undervalue the service rendered by Mr. Arnold to the Bible by the view of it which he has presented in so attractive a garb. Still less do I desire to undervalue the Bible viewed simply as a book, such as he makes it—a book which is pervaded by a noble passion for righteousness and by an in-tense belief in the reality of a moral order of the world. Whatever more may be said of the Bible, it is certainly true that it possesses these characteristics in a degree altogether unique. The Bible stands alone among books for the emphatic and persistent way in which it exalts morality, righteousness, to the sov-ereign place among human interests, and for the glowing eloquence with which in all its parts it de-clares the truth that verily there is a reward for the righteous, and a God that judgeth upon the earth; and on this account it must ever continue to com-mand the reverent respect of all morally earnest men, whatever their theological position. But the question stands over, whether Mr. Arnold, in directing atten-tion to these characteristics, has given a full account of the Bible, or has even pointed out its chief peculi-arity. In connection with that, another question has to be asked, viz., whether miracles can, as Mr. Arnold alleges, be removed from the Bible without material injury to its utility, or without affecting our conception of its chief end. "There is nothing," says this author, "one would more desire for a person or document one greatly values, than to make them independent of miracles. And with regard to the Old Testament we have done this, for we have shown that the essential matter in the Old Testament is the revelation to Israel of the immeasurable grandeur, the eternal necessity, the priceless blessing of that with which not less than three-fourths of human life is indeed concerned, righteousness. And it makes no difference to the preciousness of this revelation whether we believe that the Red Sea miraculously opened a passage to the Israelites, and the walls of Jericho miraculously fell down at the blast of Joshua's trumpet, or that these stories arose in the same way as other stories of the kind."[*] I am not careful to dispute this statement. But suppose the Bible as it stands contains another idea even more characteristic than the one Mr. Arnold signalizes, an idea to which miracle,—not, of course, this or that miracle, but a miraculous element,—is essential. In that case, to omit miracles, will simply signify changing the very fact-basis, on which our theory of revelation rests. The Bible may still contain much edifying matter, but it will be an entirely different book. It will convey different ideas from the actual Bible concerning God, man, and the world and their relations; that is to say, it will teach by implication a different theory of the universe. The mutilated Bible will suggest a

---

[*] " Literature and Dogma," pp. 123, 124.

different view of the *raison d'être* of its own existence, so different that it will be as it were the play of
Hamlet without the part of Hamlet. That there is
such an idea in the Bible I believe, and in the next
chapter I will endeavour to explain what it is.

THE CHIEF DESIGN OF REVELATION.

CHAPTER II.

THE CHIEF DESIGN OF REVELATION.

IN proceeding now to explain my view as to the chief design of revelation, it may be well to preface the discussion with a few remarks on the sense to be attached to the term Revelation. In last chapter I hinted parenthetically that Revelation and the Bible are not to be identified, as if the two terms were in all respects synonymous, and I may now briefly state the grounds of that opinion. There are then certain advantages to be gained from keeping in view the distinction between Revelation and Scripture, while, of course, ever recognising their intimate relations to each other. In the first place, the formal and deliberate recognition of the distinction may help us to wean ourselves from the one-sided doctrinaire conception of revelation which has so extensively prevailed in past times. Then, further, if once we get it into our mind, that Revelation is one thing, Scripture another, though closely related, thing, being in truth its record, interpretation, and reflection, it will help to make us independent of questions concerning the dates of books. When the various parts of the Bible were written, is an obscure and difficult ques-

tion on which much learned debate has taken place,
and is still going on; and we must be content to let
the debate run its course, for it will not be stopped
either by our wishes or by ecclesiastical authority.
And one thing which will help us to be patient, is a
clear perception that the order in which revelation
was given is to be distinguished from the order in
which the books which contain the record thereof
were written. It is conceivable that revelations might
be given in the inverse order to that in which they
were recorded. Thus, *e.g.*, a certain school of critics
tells us that the more important prophetic writings
are of earlier date than the legal portions of the
Pentateuch ; that in fact, so far as the literary record
of revelation goes, the Prophets were before the Law,
not after it, as the familiar phrase, " the Law and the
Prophets," implies. But the law may have preceded
prophecy in revelation though not in writing; in
which case not only will the phrase " Law and
Prophets " still have its truth, but, what is of much
more importance, the natural order of sequence will
be observed in the Bible history of the course of revelation.

But a still more important advantage than either
of the foregoing is to be reaped from keeping in view
the distinction in question. It is this, that the distinction makes room for the idea that possibly the
revelation which God has made to men consisted, not
in words exclusively, or even chiefly, but in deeds as
well, yea in deeds above all, forming, when connected
together, a very remarkable history. What if the
most appropriate formula for the act of revelation
were, not, " Thus saith the Lord," but " Thus did the

Lord"? In that case we could imagine a very important revelation taking place, and entering as a divine element into human history, without such a book as the Bible coming into existence at all. A book is not necessary to the being of a revelation. It may be necessary to its well-being, that it is, to insure that the revelation shall accomplish the ends for which it was given; though here we do well to bear in mind the caution of Bishop Butler, that we are no judges whether a revelation not committed to writing would or would not have answered its purpose. As an antidote to the tendency of believing minds to pronounce dogmatically on such questions, he remarks very pertinently: " I ask, What purpose? It would not have answered all the purposes which it has now answered, and in the same degree; but it would have answered others, or the same in different degrees. And which of these were the purposes of God, and best fell in with His general government, we could not at all have determined beforehand."* But without pressing such considerations, it may be admitted that a record of revelation of some sort, oral or written, was indispensable; though there is truth in the remark of Rothe, that " Divine revelation works on incessantly as co-efficient in all human knowledge, independently of its being known and recognised as revelation."† It may further be admitted that an oral record, by means of one generation showing God's works to another, is so liable to corruption, that a written record may be pronounced, in the language of the Westminster Confession, " most

---

* " Analogy," Part II., chap. iii.   † " Zur Dogmatik," p. 78.

necessary"; * that is to say, of such a high degree of utility as amounts to a practical necessity. My present object is not, of course, to disparage the value of Holy Scripture, but to assert the possibility of a revelation without a Bible, and that in the interest of a conception of revelation to which the Bible itself does ample justice, and which alone enables us to do full justice to the Bible. Put the book foremost in your idea of revelation, and you almost inevitably think of revelation as consisting in words, doctrines. Put it in the background for a moment, forget at this stage that there is a book, and you make room in your mind for the idea that revelation may proceed by acts as well as words, even more characteristically than by words. It is very necessary that we should have this idea in our minds in advancing to the consideration of the question, What is the chief end of revelation? for it will appear that that end was such as to demand Divine self-manifestation by action, not to the exclusion of words, but by action very specially —by acts of the miraculous order largely, such as those which Mr. Arnold thinks he can eliminate from the Bible without detriment to its practical value.

Revelation, then, does not mean causing a sacred book to be written for the religious instruction of mankind. What then does it mean? It signifies God manifesting Himself in the history of the world in a supernatural manner and for a special purpose. Manifesting *Himself;* for the proper subject of revelation is God. The Revealer is also the Revealed. This is recognised in the words of the Westminster Confession: "It pleased the Lord to reveal Himself,

* Chapter i. 1.

and to declare that His will unto His church."* Manifesting Himself in *history*, I add, to distinguish the
revelation now under discussion from that which God
has made of Himself in *Nature*. The words, "in a
supernatural manner and for a special purpose," are
included in the definition to distinguish the subject
under consideration from that revelation of God as a
moral Governor which is discernible in the ordinary
course of Providence. I believe that we have the
record of such a special revelation in the Bible, and
the question I have undertaken to discuss is, What is
its nature and design? In other words: If revelation in
general signify Divine self-manifestation, under what
aspect did God manifest Himself in that revelation
whereof we have a record in the Holy Scriptures?

To that question my reply is: The revelation
recorded in the Scriptures is before all things a self-
manifestation of God, as the God of *grace*. In that
revelation God appears as one who cherishes a
gracious purpose towards the human race. The revelation consists, not in the mere intimation of the
purpose, but more especially in the slow but steadfast
execution of it by a connected series of transactions
which all point in one direction, and at length reach
their goal in the realization of the end contemplated
from the first. As has been well said: "If we have
any revelation from God at all, we have it at the heart
of a great historical development; and if we are to
find the evidence of it anywhere, we must seek for it
as the cause and vital force of historical movements
and events which otherwise would never have arisen,
or, at least, would not have assumed their special

* Chapter i. 1.

shape and significance."* The animating soul of this historical movement was a purpose of grace, in which, as eventually became apparent, all mankind was concerned. though the fact was hid during the ages of preparation. But as the word "grace" is in certain departments of theology associated with very mysterious ideas, I must be careful to clear it as much as possible of associations fitted to create a prejudice at this stage. It is used here in a very simple, intelligible sense, which can be easily defined by a form of expression antithetical to that employed by Mr. Arnold to define his idea of God. Mr. Arnold describes God as "a Power not ourselves, making for righteousness." When we speak of God as the God of grace, we mean to represent Him as a Power not ourselves, making for *mercy ;* a Power that dealeth not with men after their sins, but overcometh evil with good ; a Power acting as a redeeming, healing influence on the moral and spiritual disease of the world. This is assuredly a God-worthy representation. Grace, so defined, is indeed the highest category under which we can think of God. It rises as much above righteousness as righteousness rises above the category under which natural religion conceives God, that, viz., of Might directed by intelligence. A God of righteousness is certainly a great advance on a God of mere power ; yet it is only a step upwards towards a higher idea of God, in which the Divine

---

* Smyth, "Old Faith in New Lights," p. 37. This is an admirable, and on the whole very successful attempt to adjust the apologetic argument to the modern idea of Evolution, as applied in science and in criticism. (Scribner & Co., New York).

Being becomes Self-communicating Redeeming Love.* God cannot be said to have been fully revealed till He has been revealed in this aspect. And as God has manifested Himself in nature as Power controlled by intelligence, and in the moral order of the world as a Righteous Ruler, so we should expect to find Him revealing Himself as a loving Father or gracious Redeemer. It cannot be denied that such a revelation is very much needed. The moral condition of the human race makes it very desirable. I speak of that condition simply as it reveals itself to observation, without assuming that we know anything of its cause. The doctrine of a Fall may or may not be true; at present, I do not care or need to know. However sin came into the world, the fact is, it is here, bringing manifold misery in its train. And on any theory as to the origin of sin, it is very desirable that it should, if possible, be cast out, and the manifold evils it has caused be cured. It were eminently worthy of God to undertake the task; and that He should undertake it is not only conceivable, but probable. What more worthy of God, and therefore what more likely, than that He, looking down on a race enveloped in moral darkness and corruption, should be moved with compassion, and resolve to do all that is possible to dispel the darkness by communicating the knowledge of Himself, and to remove the corruption by measures fitted to elevate and purify? And if man's state creates a need for a revelation of grace, it cannot be said that Nature or ordinary Providence supplies all the revelation that is required.

* Vid. Schweitzer, "Glaubenslehre," vol. i., p. 311.

4

It is true, indeed, as Bishop Butler has pointed out, —for few things have escaped him,—that there is a kind of rudimentary Gospel even in nature, hints that the God who made the world is one in whom a compassionate spirit dwells, and dim foreshadowings of a higher kingdom in which grace exercises free sway.* Health injured by folly can, within certain limits, be recovered; diseases have their remedies, some known, more perhaps as yet unknown; broken bones knit again.   Many such things there are to remind us that the constitution of nature is on the side of mercy, and that when men talk of the inexorable way in which natural law works on, inflicting penalties for transgression irrespective of all changes of mind on the part of the transgressor, they are only looking at one side of a matter which has two sides.   In like manner it may be said of the moral order of the world, that it is not merely a Power making for righteousness and against unrighteousness,—that is to say, playing the part of a retributive justice,—but moreover, a Power that dealeth not with men after their sins, but is merciful and gracious, and slow to anger, and repenteth of the evil threatened.   Some of the Scripture declarations to this effect concerning God, are simply readings off from the phenomena presented by ordinary Providence.   Still, while all this is to be thankfully acknowledged, it remains true that the Gospel in Nature and in ordinary Providence is very dim and rudimentary.   It is but the starlight of Divine Love, and casts only a faint ray of hope on the moral destiny of man.   The revelation of grace in

* "Analogy," Part II. chap. v.

these lower spheres comes far short of *gracious possibilities.* We can conceive manifestations of grace far
in excess of those vouchsafed in the order of nature
or in the history of nations. These lower manifestations, far from contenting us, only make us long for
something more unmistakable in intention and more
effective in influence, and inspire in our souls the hope
that, the dim starlight of grace having been given, the
sunlight will not be withheld.

To no one who accepts the theistic view of the
universe ought the fulfilment of this hope to seem incredible. We know, of course, that such an expecta-
tion must appear a dream to the thorough-going advocates of philosophic naturalism. Such a Divine
self-manifestation as is the object of the hope, is impossible except on a conception of God which naturalism disallows. Moreover, the end for which the
manifestation takes place,—the redemption of man,
the cure of moral evil,—appears from the same view-
point unattainable. It was one of the chief objections of Celsus to the Incarnation, that it had in view
an unattainable purpose. Moral evil, he said, springs
from a necessity of nature, having its origin in matter,
and its amount is constant and invariable. Even if
temporary amelioration were practicable, it is hardly
worth the trouble, for all things are subject to the
law of periodicity. That which has been shall be.
The present state of things will reproduce itself in
some future æon—any present state of things you
choose to think of. As Origen remarked, this doctrine, if true, is manifestly subversive of Christianity,
for it is idle to speak of a redemptive economy acting
on free agents by moral influences, where a reign of

necessity obtains; and if all things must eventually return to the state they were once in, then man's unredeemed state must have its turn, and Christ shall have died in vain. Modern naturalistic philosophy, whether pessimistic or optimistic in tendency, equally excludes the idea of redemption in any real sense of the word. The pessimist denies, not only that the world can be made better by any outside influence, but even that it has any inherent tendency to grow better. Things in general, and men in particular, are going on from bad to worse; and the only deliverance possible from the moral and physical evil so widely prevalent, is that the universe should cease to exist. Optimistic naturalism takes a more cheerful view of the situation. There is a steady progress onwards in the universe of being, both in the physical and in the moral sphere. The world, says Strauss, is not planned by a highest reason, but it has the highest reason for its goal. In like manner it may be, and by Strauss and others is, admitted that the tendency in the moral sphere is towards an ever increasing realization of the ideal moral order. But this hope for the future, as cherished by atheistic evolutionists, is not based on any belief in a Divine influence, or even in the free exercise of his moral faculties by man. To such thinkers, man is not a free being; and his moral improvement, if it deserves the name, is the result of the upward tendency of all surrounding cosmic influences.

No one who believes that there is a God, and that man is a moral personality, will rest satisfied with this theory of redemption by a purely physical evolution. However naturalistic in tendency, however much influenced by the sceptical spirit of the age, he will strive to hold fast, though it were in the baldest form, the idea of a redemption—a moral amelioration, springing out of influences that can be traced up to God as their source, and that act on man's reason and will and better inclinations. Repudiating all belief in supernatural grace, in the sense of the creeds, as a source of moral regeneration, and in an objective Atonement, he will yet base his hope for the transformation of human character, not only on the elements of good to be found even in the most depraved, and on the beneficent constitution of the universe acting on these from without, and provoking them into conflict with the evil within, and otherwise influencing men for good even when they are unconscious of it, but on "the action of the Divine idea, as the Gospel presents it, upon the reason of man—the idea given in that revelation of the Divine good-will, or paternal relation towards us, by which Christ has reinforced our better nature, enabling us to be intelligent fellow-workers with God in our conflict with evil, and giving a higher aim to our life."* From the orthodox point of view this is certainly a very unsatisfactory account of the renovating power of Christianity; indeed, a more meagre and colourless theory of Redemption it is hardly possible to conceive. It contains, however, one thing in advance of optimistic evolutionism, viz., the recognition of the inspiring influence of the Christian idea of God, as a God of love, or, in relation to sin, a God of grace. This idea the advocates of the theory call a revelation, in the sense that Christ, by

---

* *Vide* " Scotch Sermons." Sermon X., on *The Renovating Power of Christianity*. By the Rev. William Mackintosh, D.D.

His superior insight, for the first time discovered the import of the fact that the tendency of the influences by which we are surrounded in this world is on the whole in favour of good, rather than of evil. This tendency they regard as a feature impressed by God on the creation, and as an evidence of His design to secure the triumph of what is good, and to deliver men from the power of evil. And it is regarded as Christ's great merit, to have proclaimed to the world the significance of this divinely originated beneficent constitution of things. "After being hidden from human vision for long ages, or only partially surmised by other teachers, this design was at length brought fully to light, and presented to our faith by the Founder of Christianity."* The merit of this theory, in the eyes of modern culture, will be, that it reduces the fact-basis of its doctrine of redemption to something which can be acknowledged by men of all creeds, theistic or atheistic, provided they are not pessimists. What it builds on that fact-basis is the inspiring elevating power that lies in conceiving of the Author of the beneficent constitution of the universe as a *Father*. And without doubt there is much in a name; yet it is questionable whether it be worth while formulating a distinctive doctrine of renovation, when it differs in nothing but a name from the creed of Agnosticism. Strauss believed in the beneficent tendencies of the Universum. What great difference does it make whether I call the stream of tendency *Universum* or *Father?* The one name is warmer than the other, that is all. Every one whose mind is not completely

---

* " Scotch Sermons." Sermon X.

dominated by the naturalistic spirit of the age, will turn from so bald a doctrine in quest of a theory that shall fill the word *grace* with more meaning, and bring to bear on man a more powerful force tending towards the improvement of his moral condition.

We rise at least one degree in our idea of a revelation of grace, when we see in Christ, not merely one who read off accurately the beneficent tendency of the universe, for the enlightenment of mankind, but one who in His own person presented to view at once the ideal of humanity perfectly realised, and the fulness of Divine grace. If Christ be the sinless man, and if,—in His wondrous sympathy with the sinful, which made Him love them in spite of their moral loathesomeness, and hope for their repentance when others despaired,—He be the revealer, or exegete of the very inmost Spirit of God, then He is in a most real sense a supernatural self-manifestation of God as the God of grace. A sinless man is a moral miracle ; and the gift of him to the world is an act of creative power in which grace is revealed, because the aim of the gift is to show to men their own ideal, that by it, hovering above them in peerless excellence, they may be drawn upwards to the heights of virtue. A man full of love to the sinful, though personally sinless, is still more emphatically a revelation of grace, because in him God makes known to men for their comfort the depths of pity for the guilty hidden in the Divine bosom. Such a man, sinless yet sympathetic, awakens in me many emotions fitted to act as motives to virtue. As an ideal, he excites admiration and aspiration, and likewise shame, sorrow, humiliation, in view of my moral shortcoming, revealed to my view in darkest colours by the contrast between his character and my own.   As a sympathetic friend and brother, he quickens in the breast of a penitent hope, at the moment when he is prone to give way to despair. What more likely than that such a man should be sent into the world in the course of the ages, to be at once the crown of the first creation, and the starting point of a new career of infinite hope for mankind, the head of a new humanity?   And what more worthy of God than to undertake in good time the work of preparing the world for the advent of such a divinely endowed Man, so that he might come when and where the human race was in the fittest condition to receive and retain his beneficent influence ; determining, *e.g.,* the people out of which he should spring, and so guiding their history that he should receive from them the maximum of endowment capable of being transmitted by the law of heredity, and should find in them the best possible leverage for acting on the world?   Would not such an historical preparation for the advent of the Divine Man be a veritable revelation of grace, natural in its gradual progress, yet supernatural in its immanent aim ?   And would not the Man, when he came, be a fitting consummation to such a divinely guided process?

In these sentences I have sketched a theory of a supernatural revelation of grace, based on such a conception of the person of Christ as that contained in the Christology of Schleiermacher.   It is a theory which reduces the amount of the miraculous element in revelation to a minimum, for it regards Christ only as a sinless Man in whom the Spirit of God dwelt in the fullest possible measure.   It is also a theory which introduces the least possible amount of mystery into the nature of the influence exercised by Christ as Redeemer. He works on the world as a redeeming power by example and by sympathy, by ethical as distinct from what Schleiermacher characterized as magical influence. But in proportion as this theory gains in rationality, so to speak, it loses in motive power. For by its conception of Christ as the Ideal Man, it excludes from the number of redeeming influences the *power of God in self-sacrifice,* which can enter only with faith in the *Incarnation.* When Christ is regarded as a Divine Being entering into humanity with a redeeming purpose in His heart, we then see in God a Being subjected to sorrow by human sins, and compelled by the instincts and yearnings of His love to become a burden-bearer to His own creatures. And through such a view of God alone do we begin to comprehend what a revelation of grace means. For now we see grace revealing itself, not merely by word, through a doctrine concerning God taught by a prophet, or by Christ, to the effect that He is a Father, and that the essence of His being is love—not by word alone, but by act. And that is germane to the nature of grace. It is of the nature of true love to reveal itself by deeds as well as words. It is only feigned love that speaks kind words without corresponding actions. Grace revealed in doctrine is of value only as the promise of a higher revelation, in which all gracious possibilities shall be realised ; and only in God subjecting Himself to sacrifice are these possibilities realised. Till I see that spectacle, I can always imagine something higher; but when I see it, I perceive that the limit of gracious possibility is touched. In

4*

the Cross the revelation of grace reaches its culmination. And just because it does so, I feel that the Incarnation which makes this result possible is credible, notwithstanding the mystery and the miracle involved in the event. It is inconsistent for any one who believes grace or love to be a real attribute of God, to stumble at the supernatural in revelation; for the exclusion simply makes it impossible for the Divine Being to manifest Himself as the God of grace to the full extent of what is involved in the idea of grace. Yet with such inconsistency many in our day are chargeable who are emphatic in their proclamation of the Fatherhood of God, yet accept the philosophic doctrine of Divine immanence which makes God a prisoner in nature, unable in any case or for any reason to break through the chain of natural causality.

Thus Mr. Rathbone Greg, listening to the voice of his heart or his moral consciousness,—the sole source of revelation to the school he belongs to, that of modern speculative Theism,—feels constrained to think of God as a Personal Fatherly Being. "Strauss's Universum," he tells us, "Comte's Humanity, even Mr. Arnold's stream of tendency that makes for righteousness, excite in me no worship. I cannot pray to the 'Immensities' and the 'Eternities' of Carlyle. They proffer me no help, they vouchsafe no sympathy, they suggest no comfort. It may be that such a personal God is a mere anthropomorphic creation. But at least in resting in it, I rest in something I almost seem to realize; at least I share the view which Jesus indisputably held of the Father whom He obeyed, communed with and worshipped."* The

* "Creed of Christendom." Introduction, p. xc., 3rd ed.

words are full of interest, both for the pathetic indi-
cation which they give of the craving of the human
heart for a living God with whom it can have real
communion, even when the intellect is clouded with
doubt, and also for the incidental evidence they afford
of the unreliableness of the moral consciousness as a
source of revelation concerning Divine things. But
at least, if the moral consciousness is to be the source
of revelation, let it be used consistently. If at the
bidding of the heart I am to believe in a God who is
a Person, why not at its bidding also believe in a God
who is not imprisoned in the world, but can hear
prayer, exercise a Providence over all, do miracles,
become man, demonstrate His grace by entering into
the measures of humanity and passing through a cur-
riculum of temptation and suffering? If God is to be
personal, free, good, let Him be it out and out. I
desire a God at liberty to do heroic things, to humble
Himself.

Miss Cobbe, another representative of the same
school,—on the authority of the same oracle, the
moral consciousness,—declares that God is good, and
good in our sense of the word. Very well ; I accept
the dictum cordially, and I point in proof of its truth
to the grace of our Lord Jesus Christ who, being rich,
for our sakes became poor. Modern Theism, with its
doctrine of immanence, can point to nothing like that
in proof that God is love in the human sense of the
word. A God imprisoned in the world has no career
for self-sacrifice, that is, He cannot be love as we understand love ; for love among men shows itself most
reliably and conspicuously by self-sacrifice for the
good of others.

If the Incarnation of God for the purpose of acting as a redemptive power in the moral world be, as we have just seen, intrinsically probable on the principles of Theism, there is little room for doubt as to the fitness of Divine self-sacrifice to be a mighty force making for the regeneration of mankind. Therein indeed lies a very power of God unto salvation in all who believe. This may be confidently affirmed, quite irrespective of all questions as to rival theories of atonement. The truth of the statement rests on no special theory as to the theological significance of Christ's death, but simply on the fact that the passion of the Saviour was the passion of Deity. Admit that fact, and put on it any theological construction you please,—find in it an objective atonement for sin, or only a magnificent demonstration of self-sacrificing love intended to act on the minds of men as an ethical influence ; in either case it cannot but prove a truly Divine power making for redemption. The history of the Christian Church supplies sufficient evidence on that score, in the form of multitudes in every age turned from sin to righteousness, turned, not by particular theories of atonement, but by the great broad fact that the Son of God suffered on the cross for man's sin. The question as to the right theoretical construction to be put on that fact belongs to Biblical theology, and is simply a question of interpretation. The apologist has no vital interest in the decision. The chief consideration biassing him in favour of the theological doctrine of an *object-ive* Atonement, is that, whereas, on the ethical influence theory, Christ's power to act on the world as Redeemer is limited to those who become acquainted with His history, on this view Christ's atoning death becomes valid for all time as a sacrifice offered by the Eternal Spirit of holy love, and may exercise an important influence on the destinies of the generations which lived before His advent, as well as on those which came after, and of those who have never heard His name, as well as on those to whom the Gospel has been preached. Those who deny an objective Atonement, simply cancel the Godward aspect of Christ's self-sacrifice; the human aspect of unspeakable sympathy and love, taking on itself the burden of the world's sin and misery, remains, with all the ethical power to change the current of the moral affections and to inspire enthusiastic devotion to the Divine kingdom.

But the question still remains, whether the Scriptures, which purport to be the records of revelation, bear out the view I have given as to the chief end for which a revelation was vouchsafed. Does the literature of the Bible, on thoughtful perusal, convey the impression that its contents chiefly relate to a *purpose of grace*, and that its great watchword is *redemption?* Now there can be no hesitation as to the answer to be given to this question, so far as the New Testament is concerned. Christianity, the New Testament being witness, is emphatically and before all things the religion of redemption. Mr. Arnold sums up Christ's teaching in two sentences: "Seek thy happiness from within, not from without"; and, "that thou mayest be happy, thou must deny thyself." Christ did say these things; but He had a great deal more to say than they amount to. There are other sayings even more characteristic of His doctrine, and more instructive as to the nature of His mission ; two in particular. These are : " The Son of Man is come to save that which was lost," and " The Kingdom of heaven is at hand." The former saying, often uttered by Jesus, implies that His mission had special reference to the sinful ; and in accordance with this we find from the Gospel records that He spent much of His time among people belonging to the degraded classes of Jewish society. This part of His conduct, as all know, was much misunderstood, and gave frequent occasion for faultfinding, whereby He was put on His defence. The defences He offered were very striking, very beautiful, and very instructive as to the nature of the religion which He came to inaugurate. He said at one time, " They that be whole need not a Physician, but they that are sick," to signify that Christianity is a religion of redemption, and therefore busies itself fitly with those who most urgently need remedy. At another time He said in effect, " To whom much is forgiven the same loveth much," to teach that Christianity not only occupies itself with the sinful, but has an interest in taking pains to make converts from among the greatest offenders, because among these it finds the greatest capacity of devotion. On a third occasion He said, " There is joy in heaven over one sinner repenting, more than over ninety and nine just persons who need no repentance," to intimate that in the view of Christianity the meanest of mankind was worth saving ; the repentance of even a poor publican (for such a case was in Christ's view when He spake the saying quoted) an event of solemn interest, and a most fitting occasion of gladness. From these golden words it is evident that Christ's

mission, in His own view, was, before all, that of a
spiritual Healer. And without going into details, for
which there is no space, I may remark, that from all
our Lord's recorded utterances, it appears that the
Kingdom He proclaimed was a Kingdom of grace,
open to all on condition of faith and repentance—a
Kingdom whose advent was good news, and which
was itself the *summum bonum*, because therein God
in His Paternal Benignity admitted men freely forgiven to unrestricted fellowship with Himself, and
so united them in fraternal bonds to each other as
members of a holy commonwealth. Christ's teaching on both heads, the nature of His own mission and
the nature of the Kingdom, was thus full of grace, as
He Himself was full of grace, as the Friend of sinners
and Redeemer of men.

In the Pauline conception of Christianity it is not
less conspicuously the religion of redemption. Paul
indeed seems constantly to be occupied with the idea
of *righteousness ;* but righteousness in his pages is
really a synonym for grace. The righteousness of the
Pauline epistles is usually, though not invariably, an
objective righteousness, not in us, but hovering over
us, a gift of Divine grace, the righteousness of God
given to faith. This may seem a very artificial idea
of righteousness, but that is a question of words ; the
thing which Paul is ever thinking of is the grace of
God that bringeth salvation. The Master and the
Apostle in their respective types of doctrine coincide
in the main. They certainly contemplate the same
thing, the *summum bonum*, from different points of
view ; but it is the same thing both have in their
eye ; and even the respective view-points, as we shall

see hereafter, are more closely related than they
seem.*

As Paul read the Old Testament, it also had to do
above all things with redemption or the purpose of
grace. The chief thing he found there, the kernel or
hidden treasure of the Hebrew Scriptures, was the
revelation of the Promise. To the ordinary Jew the
Law appeared the principal matter, the promise re-
tiring into the background, recognised doubtless as
the end to be reached by the keeping of the law as
the means, but completely overshadowed by the importance attached to the means. But Paul inverted
the order of importance, and vindicated for the promise the place of supremacy. Before the law in time,
it was therefore also entitled to come after it, super-
seding it when it had served its temporary purpose,
which was simply to prepare the race of Abraham and
the world generally, in its minority, for the enjoyment
of the promise when the heir entered on his majority,
and became at length a genuine Son of God.

Was Paul's reading of the Old Testament correct,
or did he read into it a system of ideas not really
there, revealed to his mind, not by legitimate exegesis,
but by a peculiar religious experience? *Primâ facie*
the latter may appear to be the true state of the case.
Pfleiderer accordingly affirms that the Apostle's view
of the relation between the law and the promise " was
quite remote from the historical intention of the lawgiving, and wholly without ground in the letter of the
law." " It is," he says, " for the consciousness which

---

* Some further observations on Christ's doctrine and Paul's concerning the gift of grace, as compared with each other, will be
found in chapter vi. of this work.

takes its stand on the historical soil of the Old Testament, simply a matter of course, that the law would not be given in order to increase sin through its non-fulfilment, but in order to be fulfilled, and so to lead to righteousness. Nor could it appear to such a consciousness that this aim of the law stood in any opposition to the promise to Abraham; on the contrary, it would appear to him a matter of course that God gave to Abraham the blessing on the understanding that the seed of Abraham was to render obedience to the Divine will, in other words to the law afterwards to be given."* Now probably such were the thoughts of men at the beginning; but this does not settle the question of the Divine intention in the lawgiving. We must distinguish between the Divine end of the law, and the end which was present to the minds of the instruments of revelation, *e.g.* Moses. From the point of view of Divine teleology the Apostle's doctrine of the law is unassailable. The ultimate result reveals the initial Divine intention, so that we may say that what God had in view from the first was the promise, and that the law entered to prepare men for the reception of the promised blessing by a varied discipline, to be a pedagogue, a gaoler, a tutor, and a rough husband, to make Christ and the era of grace, liberty, and love welcome. The law was a lower stage in the development of humanity, preparing for a higher, in presence of which it loses its rights, though the good that was in it is taken up into the higher, and united to the initial stage of the promise to which it stood in opposition. But as for the thoughts of the Jewish

* "Paulinismus," p. 87.

legislator and his contemporaries and successors belonging to the early generations of Israel's history,
they may have been considerably different from those
of Paul, who contemplated the matter in view of the
result.   They looked with hope on an institution
which was destined to end in failure and despair. The
commandment which Paul found to be unto death,
they regarded as ordained unto life.   They did not
see to the end of that which was to be abolished;
there was a veil upon their faces in reference to the
purpose of the law.   It was only as time went on that
the veil began to be taken away by sorrowful experiences, and spirit-taught souls began to see that the
commandment was ordained, not so much for life and
blessedness, as for the knowledge of sin and misery;
and that if any good was to come to Israel, it must
be by the supersession of the Sinaitic covenant through
a new covenant of grace, under which the law should
be written, not on tables of stone, but on the heart,
and all iniquity should be freely forgiven.

Keeping in view the slow and gradual manner in
which even inspired men attained to a comprehension
of the Divine purpose in the lawgiving, we should
not be surprised were there found not a little in the
Old Testament to bear out the impression that righteousness in a legal sense is its burthen. We should
not even be surprised to find not a few traces of the
influence of a legal *spirit* in the literature of the Old
Covenant; for what would these prove but this, that
the child's thoughts during the period of tutors and
governors were tinged by the discipline under which
he lived?   That such traces are to be found we shall
see hereafter.   But when due allowance has been

made for these, it still remains true that the keynote
of the Old Testament is grace, and that the deepest
current of thought runs in the direction of a religion
of Trust in God as the Redeemer. If one wanted a
single text which should most faithfully indicate the
general drift of the Hebrew Scriptures, he might not
inaptly find it in the beautiful words of the later
Isaiah: "Doubtless Thou art our Father, though
Abraham be ignorant of us, and Israel acknowledge
us not: Thou, O Lord, art our Father, our Redeemer
from everlasting is Thy name." So far is legal righteousness from being the deepest thought of the Old
Testament writers, that the word righteousness itself
is often used by them, as by Paul, as a synonym for
grace, or for God's faithfulness in keeping His promise; as in the words of the hundred and third Psalm:
"The mercy of the Lord is from everlasting to everlasting upon them that fear Him, and His righteousness unto children's children." Nor is this a solitary
text; similar utterances abound in the sacred books,
insomuch that some go the length of affirming that
the word righteousness is scarcely ever used in the
sense of retributive justice, but almost always is practically synonymous with grace.

The idea of grace is very conspicuous in the prophetic literature. The God of the great prophets
Jeremiah, Ezekiel, and the author of the later portions
of the book of *Isaiah's* prophecies, as also very specially
of *Hosea,* is characteristically a God who assumes a
gracious attitude towards His people, as the forgiver
of Israel's iniquities, the healer of her spiritual diseases, the founder of a new covenant which shall be
free from the faults adhering to the old one. And

along with this evangelic idea of God goes a certain universalism, a recognition of the truth that Israel has not a monopoly of God's grace, that its benefits are open to all. The God who is the Redeemer of Israel, addresses the whole world in these terms: "Look unto Me and be ye saved, all the ends of the earth, for I am God, and there is none else." Israel is regarded as elected to be a missionary people to spread the knowledge of the true God among the nations, and so to make her God the ground of her claim to the gratitude and respect of mankind. This is only what we should expect; for a religion of grace recognizes no claim in ·any man or people to Divine favour as matter of right, and therefore consistently puts all men and nations on the same level. Such a religion may not deny absolutely the prerogatives of a particular people like Israel as an elect race; but it will make these prerogatives consist in being the vehicle through which God conveys His grace to all others, and so regard election as merely a method by which God uses the few to bless the many.

These remarks remind us that in the Scripture account of Abraham's history God is represented as addressing to the Patriarch a call in which the prophetic conception of God and of Israel's destiny is already anticipated. That call contained the promise: "I will make of thee a great nation, and I will bless thee, and make thy name great; and thou shalt be a blessing: and in thee shall all families of the earth be blessed." The words throughout are full of grace. God's attitude is that of one who sovereignly and freely blesses; whether the blessing be temporal or spiritual does not matter, the spirit is the same in

either case. They are also pervaded by the spirit of
universalism. The God who is to bless Abraham and
his descendants means also to bless all nations; means
to bless them by blessing Abraham and his offspring.
This holds true whether we retain the version of the
last clause of the above text, given in the English
Bible, or accept that proposed by critics: " In thee
shall all families of the earth bless themselves." The
nations could bless themselves in Israel only because
they knew and appreciated her state ; and those who
could do this would be themselves partakers of the
blessing.

If such a promise was really made to Abraham, if
he left his native abode with such a hope in his
breast, then it may be truly said that the revelation
recorded in the Bible from its very commencement
was a revelation of grace. In a sense it may be said
that the Bible begins with the call of Abraham, all
that goes before, the first eleven chapters of Genesis,
being a preface intended to convey a general idea of
the state of the world when the progenitor of Israel
came upon the scene. Yet here, at the very starting
point of the history in the long course of which the
gracious purpose of the self-revealing God was to be
slowly evolved, we find the nature of the purpose
made known with a degree of clearness approaching
that with which it shines in the pages of the prophets.
But naturalistic critics tell us that there is a very simple explanation of this. The prophetic ideas of God
and of Israel's destiny are in the history of Abraham,
because the prophets put them there. " From the
hands of prophetic revisers," says Pfleiderer, " flow
those traits in the history of the origins of Israel which

throw back into the earliest foretime the Messianic hopes and the thought of a universal purpose of grace, which were both in reality mental achievements of the later centuries. We include under these particularly the treatment of the patriarchal age, and above all the life of Abraham. On this territory of dawning fore-history the prophetic narrator has operated with great freedom."[*] The assumption underlying this sceptical criticism is, that the rudimentary initial stage in a process of religious development cannot possibly anticipate the features of a more advanced stage, but must necessarily present the religious element in human nature under the rudest form. A comparatively pure monotheistic idea of God is wholly foreign to this early stage. The development which ends in ethical monotheism must start from fetish worship. In like manner the idea of a universal religion cannot possibly appear in the initial period. Universalism can come only after particularism, the worship of tribal or national gods, has had its day. Now these positions, so confidently laid down by naturalism, are by no means so axiomatic as writers like Kuenen imagine. On grounds of observation, *e.g.*, and in the interests of a purely scientific study of religion, it has been questioned whether fetishism be not rather a degenerate form of an antecedent purer religion than the primitive form of religion from which all religious development starts.[†] The truth seems to be, that the early form of all historical religions is not fetish worship, but a comparatively pure, though unstable, mo-

---

[*] "Die Religion," vol. ii., pp. 337, 338.

[†] This is the view advocated by Max Müller in his Hibbert Lectures, "On the Origin and Development of Religion."

notheism. The first thoughts of men on religion are better than their second, and their last and best thoughts are in a sense a return to their first. In accordance with this view, the initial stage of a religion may, without postulating any supernatural revelation, contain in it in germinal form all that is to come out of it. This law of development was exemplified in the case of Christ, by the admission of even rationalistic critics like Dr. Baur. Why not also in the case of Abraham, if he was the starting point of the development which culminated in the ethical monotheism and universalism of Hebrew prophecy? Why should there not appear in him the blossom of which the prophetic ideal is the ripe fruit? Is it thought that he came at too early a period in the world's history for this to be possible? But is it not the fact, demonstrated by comparative philology, that at a still earlier period the primitive Aryans worshipped the one God under the name of Dyauspitar—Heaven-Father. Why then should it seem impossible for Abraham to have a comparatively pure idea of God? Or is it the universalism of the Abrahamic creed that seems too advanced for the time? It is a well-known fact that a universal religion appeared in India some six centuries before the Christian era: why should not the dream at least of such religion appear still earlier in Chaldea? The idea of all nations being bound together and blessed by one religious faith, advanced and modern as it seems, is after all a simple thought which might readily occur to devout minds even in the grey dawn or childhood of the world's history. Wherever God is conceived of as one, there mankind also may be conceived of as one. The

ancient Aryans who looked up to heaven and said
"Father," must have looked on all men as brethren.
The instincts of human nature, even in savages, are
able to make the synthesis between one God and one
humanity. Hence Paul, in his address on Mar's hill
to Athenian polytheists, connects together the two
ideas of one God, maker of heaven and earth, and one
humanity made of one blood, evidently assuming that
the acceptance of the one idea would carry along with
it the acceptance of the other. These ideas, therefore,
cannot reasonably be regarded as too advanced for
Abraham, even regarding him as an ordinary man ;
and if we regard him as an exceptionally great man,
one of the world's epoch-making men,—and such appear in all ages,—his capacity to entertain such
thoughts becomes still more credible. Students of
history recognise in *Zoroaster* a probable contemporary of Abraham, and regard him as one who played
among his people, the Persian Aryans, the important
rôle of a religious reformer, teaching them to believe
in one God ethically conceived as the patron of righteousness, and maker of all good things in the world.*
If this view be well founded, then Zoroaster was one
of the world's great characters appearing in the morn-
ing of human history. If the Bible picture of Abraham,—in which he is represented as the introducer of
a new pure religion, as a man who by faith lived in
the future and cherished the aspiration to be a benefactor to the human race,—be even approximately
correct, then the Hebrew Patriarch is simply another
to be added to the select band of world-historical ini-
tiators.

---

* *Vide* Bunsen, "God in History," vol. i., p. 276.

But it is not necessary to ascribe so much originality to Abraham in order to vindicate for the self-
manifestation of God in history, even at his early
epoch, the character of a revelation of a purpose of
grace. At no stage in the history of revelation is it
necessary to assume a full understanding or consciousness, on the part of the instruments of revelation,
of the purposes for which God was using them; and
least of all is this probable in the initial stage. It is
distinctly indicated in the New Testament that the
prophets did not fully understand the meaning of
their own prophecies; and we may well believe that
Abraham did not possess perfect insight into the significance of the impulses that were at work in his
soul. For the purposes of our argument we can afford
to admit that the prophets, or whoever wrote the
patriarchal history, give in their narrative the Divine
significance of the events in Abraham's life, as it lay
revealed to their view by the course of Israel's history,
rather than the meaning which these bore to Abraham's own mind. It is enough for our purpose if the
main outlines of the story be historically correct:
that Abraham left his native land in search of another
place of abode, that the migration proceeded in part
at least from religious motives, and that the wanderer,
sojourning in the strange land, had a deep-seated
presentiment and hope that from him should spring
a people destined to play a remarkable part in the
history of the world. Of the import of these events
in his life, and of the feelings connected with them,
Abraham himself might have a very dim and inadequate idea. His departure from his native country
might be the result of an irresistible impulse, rather

5

than of a deliberate purpose; the religious motive might take the form, not of an altered view of God distinctly formulated by deliberate reflection, but rather of an undefinable dissatisfaction with prevalent religious beliefs and practices; the hope of founding a nation peculiar in character and vocation, might be nothing more in consciousness than a persistent presentiment of which no account could be given, a sort of fixed idea, for the cherishing of which a man might be reckoned a madman or a sage, according as the event fell out. If this were ascertained to be Abraham's actual state of mind, then it might have to be admitted that his life, as narrated in Genesis, has undergone considerable colouring in the hands of the historian. Still the *residuum* of fact would form a sufficient basis for the revelation of a Divine intention. In those facts one might see revealed a purpose of God to separate this man from his own people and to make him the progenitor of a new race which should permanently occupy the land wherein he found rest after his wanderings, and which should be there an elect people, worshippers of the true God, and destined eventually to become missionaries of the true religion to the whole earth. It was just such a Divine intention the author of the Book of Genesis, call him a prophet if you will, saw in the facts. From the point of view of such a Divine intention he wrote the history, striking the keynote in the very first sentence, which represents Jehovah as saying to Abraham : "Get thee out of thy country, and from thy kindred, and from thy father's house, unto a land that I will show thee : and I will make of thee a great nation, and I will bless thee, and make thy name great; and thou shalt be a blessing: and I will bless them that bless thee, and curse him that curseth thee: and in thee shall all families of the earth be blessed." This was what God said to Abraham, if not in so many words audible to the ear, then by the impulses which He awakened in the patriarch's heart. This was what the history of Abraham said to the prophet's own spirit. It was his way of read_ing the story, the construction which his prophetic insight taught him to put on the facts. And the event showed that the construction was right. If God be in history at all, the prophetic hypothesis is verified. The Power who is at work in the world did mean in the events of Abraham's life just what the prophetic narrator says He meant. In that life God revealed Himself as One having in view, as His end in guiding the course of history, the religious well-being of mankind, and adopting for that purpose the method of election. The revelation lies in the events themselves; the purpose served by the Bible narrative, beyond the mere recording of the facts, is to enable us to see clearly the Divine intention, to see it more clearly than we should have done, had we had nothing more than a bald statement of the facts, more clearly than the hero of the story himself saw it.

In the foregoing observations 'I have admitted that the prophetic narrative of Abraham's life puts more meaning into that life than it had or could have to Abraham. It is important to point out, however, that the amount of light thrown on the Divine intentions is not greatly if at all in excess of what we might expect in the initial stage of revelation. The narrative does not imply that Abraham possessed a per-

fectly adequate or pure idea of God, or a full knowledge as to the extent or manner of the blessing to be
conferred on him and his descendants, and through
them on the world.   As respects the former, the name
for God in the patriarchal period, while expressive of
truth so far as it goes, comes far short of the conception of God suggested by the crowning stage of revelation.   It is El-shaddai, God Almighty.*   It conveys
the idea that God is the Maker of the world, and at
the same time above the world, not to be confounded
with nature as in the Pagan religions, which practically
are but different forms of nature-worship.   The name
thus expresses a most important truth; no one can
realise how important till he has studied the religions
of the world, and observed how completely God and
nature are identified, to the utter exclusion of all right
ideas of the relations of God and the world as Creator
and creature, Maker and made.   In connection with
these studies we learn to appreciate at its due value
the revelation of God contained in the very first chapter of the Book of Genesis, which sets forth God as
the Creator of heaven and earth, independent of the
world, existing before it, bringing it into being by the
word of His power, and making man in His own image.   Still this first revelation, important as it is, is
rudimentary in comparison with that made in after
ages when the purpose of grace was more unfolded.
It amounts to little more than a publication of the
truths of natural religion, a republication, we may
call it, if we conceive of man as having received a
primitive revelation of the simple elements of religion,

---

* Gen. xvii. 1 ; Exod. vi. 3.

the light of which he afterwards lost. It tells us only at most that God is One, that He is above the world, that He made the world by His power, and that He is a Being who, in His moral nature, in some respects resembles man. Truths, these, not to be despised; nay, truths which serve for a foundation to those which more especially form the revelation of grace. Still they are nothing more than foundation; they but conduct us to the threshold of revelation proper. The *raison d'être* of revelation is not to teach us these truths. If the Book which contains the record of revelation gives to these truths a place in its pages, it is because they are presuppositions which we must bring with us to the study of the higher revelation. If the place assigned to such truths appear larger than seems due to subordinate matters, it is because men have been slow to learn even the lower truths concerning God, not to speak of the higher. That God is the Creator, and that He is a moral Governor, the sacred book asserts and reasserts, because even these truths are extensively ignored, and because till these are laid to heart it is hopeless to seek to gain recognition for the highest idea of God as a Redeemer. The inculcation of the lower truths is a means to an ulterior end; they are not taught for their own sake.

Returning from this digression, I remark that the patriarchal name for God shows that the patriarchs in their theology were still little in advance of the standing point of a purified natural religion. And when we look with a thoughtful eye into Abraham's history we find evidence that he still needed to be raised above the influence of some of the superstitions prevalent among the peoples who had not retained the true God in their knowledge. I refer specially here to what may legitimately be inferred from the narrative relating to the sacrifice of Isaac. There can be little doubt that that remarkable passage in the patriarch's history stands in some relation to the custom of human sacrifice, which was one of the most characteristic features of pagan Semitic worship, and, in the opinion of some writers, found its way into Canaan from Babylon. We may assume that Abraham was familiar with the horrid practice; and it is every way likely that the knowledge he possessed supplied the needful fulcrum for the "temptation" to which he was subjected. The fact that the votaries of Baal or Moloch, the Divine Lord and King, were ready to make their own children pass through the fire in his honour, made it possible for Abraham to entertain as a Divine suggestion or command the thought of offering his son Isaac as a sacrifice in proof of his devotion. Was it not due to his God that he should show that he loved Him more than the dearest object of affection, even though it should be an only son through whom alone he could attain to the fulfilment of his hope for the future? If he was not willing to make such a sacrifice, did he not come behind the idolaters from whom he had separated himself, in the sincerity and intensity of his religious zeal? One could imagine such questions suggesting themselves to the mind of a devout man placed in Abraham's circumstances, without any Divine communication. Supernatural interposition was needed, not so much to put the thought into Abraham's mind, as to conduct him safely through the temptation which it brought to him, and to lift him permanently above

the crude ideas of God which made such a temptation
possible. It is probably in this direction we should
look for a solution of the difficulties connected with
the moral aspects of the episode, which have so much
exercised the wits of apologists. In his able work,
" Ruling Ideas in Early Ages," the late Dr. Mozley
endeavours to vindicate the morality of the command
given to Abraham to sacrifice his son, by insisting
that it must be looked at in connection with the ideas
prevailing in that age respecting the absolute right of
fathers to dispose of the lives of their children. The
defence involves the admission that these ideas were
crude, and the morality associated with them very imperfect ; and the plea is, that God, in making a revelation, was obliged to take men up at the point where
He found them, and so gradually lead them on to
higher things. The aim of the author in the whole
argument is, to show that God could do, or command
to be done, or approve when done, in one age what
neither ought to be done in a later, more advanced
time, when men's moral ideas had undergone a change
for the better, nor could even so much as be believed
on any evidence to be the objects of Divine approbation or the subjects of Divine commands. The line
of thought is valuable and fruitful, and might be applied to other subjects, and to the same subjects in
other ways, besides those to which prominence is giv-
en in the work referred to. What Dr. Mozley empha-
sizes in the case of Abraham's offering of Isaac, is the
right of a parent, according to the ideas of the time,
to sacrifice the life of his son. It was then thought
that a man might dispose of a son as if he were a
thing, not a person ; therefore it was possible for Abra-

ham to believe on proper evidence that God required this of him ; therefore also God might in fact require it for a worthy end.   But there is more than the right to be thought of; there is the sense of obligation, the idea in Abraham's mind that he ought to slay his son as an act of religious homage, an idea present to his thoughts antecedent to any Divine command, and forming the natural basis for the whole experience to be passed through.   If we assume this idea to have been in Abraham's mind, then we cannot only under-stand the possibility of the temptation, but can see that a very definite special purpose was served beyond the general one of trying his faith—that, viz., of de-livering the patriarch finally and completely from the fascinating influence of surrounding superstitions, by showing him that his God was one who desired indeed to be loved supremely, with single-hearted devotion, but who delighted not in sacrifices of blood.   This use of the experience was perfectly compatible with the trial of faith which the narrative represents as its chief purpose.   That trial arose out of a conflict be-tween two duties—the duty, on the one hand, of of-fering up Isaac in sacrifice in obedience to a Divine command, and the duty, on the other, of continuing to believe firmly in the Divine promise.   The trial re-mains the same, on any theory as to the way in which Abraham came to be convinced that the former of the two duties was incumbent on him.   Dr. Mozley's theory is, that conviction was produced by a direct Divine command, recognisable as such by miraculous accompaniments.   The alternative theory is, that the state of Abraham's mind in reference to religion was such that conviction might come to him through the ordinary action of his conscience. In either case it might be said with truth that God spoke to him. It is only a question as to the mode of speaking; as in reference to the design of the communication, it is a question whether God meant to teach one lesson only or two—a general one, His unconditional power to fulfil His promise, and a special one, the difference between the true God and Baal in ethical character. The latter was a lesson which it was worthy of the God of revelation to teach, it was indeed a most important contribution to the self-manifestation of God as the God of grace. And it is not derogatory to the character of Abraham to suppose that he needed the lesson. To imagine him susceptible to the fascinations of Moloch worship, is not to make him "a follower and disciple of the Canaanites."* It must be borne in mind, that the very sincerity of the sojourner in the land of Canaan, as a servant of God, would tend in some ways to lay him open to the sinister influence of surrounding superstitions. The practice of human sacrifice was an expression in a perverted form of the great truth that the Divine interest must take precedence of every human interest. While regarding with horror the manner in which effect was given to the principle, the devout Hebrew could not but feel respect for the earnestness which shrunk not from the supreme test of subjection to its behests. But if such was his feeling, we can easily see the need of some special discipline to enable him to separate the spirit of devotion from the offensive form in which

---

* Dr. Mozley adduces it as an argument against the view given above, that it does so degrade Abraham.

5*

it clothed itself in prevalent religious custom; and no better can be imagined than that described in the record of his life.*

The foregoing observations go to show that Abraham's idea of God stood in need of purification and development. I now remark, that if his conception of the Divine character was imperfect, his knowledge of the Divine purpose, as judged by the record, was by no means complete. He had a presentiment that God was to bless his descendants, and through them the world; but he had but dim rudimentary ideas of the nature of the blessing to be conferred. Material things occupied a large place in his thoughts. He left his native abode in quest of a land that God was to show him; and that his seed should inherit this land was the great object of his hope. That a religious element also entered into his conception of the blessing, may be inferred from the fact that religion was one of the springs out of which the migration flowed. But we are not required by anything in the narrative to suppose that Abraham's ideas of the spiritual side of the promise were in advance of what is to be looked for at the initial stage of revelation. It was the patriarch's hope, doubtless, that his children would be sincere worshippers of the true God, the Almighty Maker of heaven and earth, and the righteous Judge of the sons of men; and he might also hope that through the people that should spring from his loins other nations would be brought to the knowledge of the same God, and thus be led to

---

* For some excellent remarks in the line of those offered in the text, see Smyth's "Old Faiths in New Light," pp. 99–104.

abandon their idols. Beyond this, however, his view
did not greatly extend. The higher truths of revelation had not yet risen above the horizon.

Yet let us not imagine on this account that revelation had not yet begun to show itself in its distinctive
proper character as a revelation of grace. The
flower, though not the fruitage of grace appeared in
the patriarchal revelation. And as the flower is a
prophecy of the fruit, it may be said that in the
flower Abraham saw unconsciously the fruit, Christ's
day, and rejoiced in it. There was grace in all God's
dealings with Abraham. It was an act of grace to
show him the falsity of the prevailing religion, and
to reveal to him the pure truth of natural religion,
the worship of God the Creator and Moral Governor.
It was a further act of grace to separate him from
his people, that he might forget old customs and, as
a stranger in a strange land, worship the true God.
There was grace also in the promise of a seed, and
of a land in which they should dwell as in a peculiar
sense a people of God. The covenant by which God
appropriated Abraham's seed as His people, and gave
Himself to them to be specially their God, was a
covenant of grace. The lesson on sacrifice was also
a remarkable manifestation of grace, for while it ne-
gatively revealed the *humanity* of the Divine character, it positively revealed God's delight in self-sacrifice, and thus brought to light possibilities of sacrifice
for God Himself, which one could hardly dare to regard even as possibilities until they had actually been
realised. The Divine oath uttered on the occasion,
as a passionate expression of the admiration awakened by the sublime spectacle presented by the patri-

arch offering up his son, is specially significant as affording a glimpse into the inmost spirit of God. Looking down on the sacrifice, God exclaims: "As I live, this is a great heroic deed; it shall not go unrewarded. Out of the son whom this man is willing to part with shall spring a seed multitudinous as the stars or the sand." He could swear by no greater, therefore He sware by Himself; so, as the writer of the Epistle to the Hebrews finely points out, making Himself a Mediator, or middle party between God and Abraham. God swearing made Himself in condescension inferior to God sworn by. That is, God, in taking an oath, did a thing analogous to God becoming man. The acts were kindred, being both acts of condescension and love. In these two acts, as in covenant-making, God stoops down from His majesty to the weakness and want and low estate of man. In covenant-making God made Himself a debtor to His creatures, and gave them a right to claim what is in reality a matter of favor. In taking an oath, God submitted to indignity imposed by man's distrust, and, instead of standing on His truth, put Himself under oath, that there might be an end of doubt or gainsaying. In becoming man, God condescended to man's sin, and submitted to be as a Sinner that sinners might be delivered from moral evil. Grace appears in all these acts in an ever ascending degree.

THE METHOD OF REVELATION.

CHAPTER III.

THE METHOD OF REVELATION.

THE chief end of revelation being to make known a purpose of grace in which all mankind were interested, it might have been expected *à priori*, that the revelation would be made at once, *per saltum*, and by miracle to all concerned. Such a purpose, one would say, can brook no delay, but must be in haste to bless its objects; can be guilty of no partiality, but must treat all with like favour; and must reach its full accomplishment, not by a slow progress from lower to higher degrees of blessing, but at a bound. The method actually pursued was as unlike this imaginary one as possible, and more in accordance with the analogy of nature and ordinary Providence. Revelation took the form of an historical movement, subject to the ordinary laws of historic development, and exhibiting the usual characteristics of movements subject to these laws. The redemptive purpose of God was not ushered into the world a full-grown fact; it evolved itself by a regular process of growth, and the process was marked by three salient features: slow movement, partial action, and advance to the perfect from the more or less imperfect, not only in knowledge, but also in morality. All these features may be and have been made the occasion of objection to the reality of a Divine revelation; and it may be worth while to consider how far they are compatible with the idea of a revelation in general, and more especially with the idea of a revelation of God as the God of Grace. The present chapter shall be devoted to the examination of this problem.

I begin the discussion with the general remark, that it ought to raise no prejudice against the divinity of an alleged revelation, that it assumes the form of an historical movement. It is worthy of God to proceed in this way. " It became Him for whom are all things, and by whom are all things," in making a special revelation, to act in accordance with the laws which He observes in making a general revelation of Himself as the Creator and Governor through nature and ordinary Providence. Adherence to this method, even in a supernatural revelation, ensures that this higher self-manifestation shall bear a stamp of naturalness, as opposed to the magical character that must attach to all Divine action which stands in no relation to the course of nature. A redemptive process from which the element of time was eliminated, would have been a thaumaturgical performance so utterly unlike the world we live in, where all things are subject to the law of growth, that it would have been hard for us, living in such a world, to believe that it could be the work of the same God who made and governs the universe. It would have been a phenomenon of the same kind as had been the deliverance of Israel out of Egypt by lifting her up and carrying her through the air to the promised land as an eagle carries her young till they have learned to fly. It so happens, indeed, that in the

song of Moses, that great historical achievement is
actually represented under this very figure: "As an
eagle stirreth up her nest," wrote the sacred poet, "flut-
tereth over her young, spreadeth abroad her wings,
taketh them, beareth them on her wings: so the Lord
alone did lead him, and there was no strange god
with him!"* And in a high ideal sense the representation is true. Yet it is only an ideal; it is poetry,
in which all secondary ordinary causes are lost sight
of, and the Divine agency alone is recognised. Nevertheless such second causes were not in reality excluded. God led His people from Egypt to Palestine
like a flock, by the hand of Moses and Aaron; and
the process was of much longer duration than the
poetic figure implies. Nor did the work of deliver-
ing Israel lose any of its divineness by being carried
on slowly and by human instrumentality. On the
contrary, it thereby only came to have a history full
of moral interest, and throwing much light on the
character of God. Had Israel been delivered in a
purely magical way, lifted up out of the land of bondage and set down a few hours after in the land of
promise, it would certainly have been a stupendous
miracle; yet it would have been a poor display of the
Divine character compared with that furnished by
the actual method. In the imaginary case we should
have seen only the Divine omnipotence manifested
for a moment; in the actual case we behold a manifestation of all the Divine attributes, power, wisdom,
patience, faithfulness, unwearied loving care—not a
momentary manifestation only, but one extending

* Deut. xxxii. 11, 12.

over a lengthened series of years, supplying material
for a history rich in pathetic stirring incident which
endures for aye, an imperishable monument to the
praise of Israel's God.

The naturalness of the way in which God redeemed
Israel, it thus appears, was far from being a fault. In
like manner the same characteristic is no fault in the
method pursued in the higher work of redemption,
whereof that of Israel in Egypt was in some respects
a type. The naturalness of that method is rather a
point in its favour, to be emphasized by the apologist
as far as the facts will allow. And we might go great
lengths in such an argument without exceeding the
limits of truth. The whole process of revelation
was so natural that it might easily seem on first view
to be nothing more. That it was something more,
that there was a supernatural element within the
natural, we shall see hereafter; meantime the thing
to be noted is, how natural, how much like an ordinary historical movement, was the course of events
through which God revealed and brought to its consummation His purpose of grace towards mankind.
In the first place, the drama of revelation begins at
the beginning, and, though it concerns the whole
human race, has to do at the starting with a single
individual. Such a commencement shows at once
how thoroughly historical the process is going to be,
for it is characteristic of great historical movements,
to begin with individuals and to expand gradually
from them as centres, or to grow up from them as
seeds, till they become at length world-wide phenomena. A revelation which begins with the call of
Abraham is evidently going to take the form of an

organic evolution, passing by a slow secular process
through successive stages till it reach its final phase;
from an individual man to a family, from a family to
a nation, from a nation to a representative Man in
whom a new beginning is made, and the universal
element for the first time clearly appears, and from
the representative Man to all the nations of the earth.
Surely a magnificent world-historical movement, extending through the ages, worthy of the first cause
and last end of all, approving itself by its very
leisureliness to be the work of Him whose mode of
action is slow but sure, never hasting, yet never for-
getting His purpose!

Yes, it may be objected, very sublime and very
God-like and God-worthy in some respects; but is the
delay involved in this method compatible with the
idea of Grace? Doubtless it is God's way, as the
Governor of the world, to work after the fashion described. The moral order of the world, as even
pagan sages discerned, moves towards its end slowly
if surely. One day is with the Lord, as a Power
making for righteousness, as a thousand years, in
respect of the leisureliness of His action; and a thousand years as one day, in respect of mindfulness of
His purpose. But ought not God, as a *Gracious*
Power to act in a different manner? Does not so
slow a movement as that which characterizes the
moral order of the world, exclude grace altogether?
Can we who believe in grace avail ourselves of this
feature of Divine action; have we not adopted an
idea of God which is inconsistent with the fact-basis?

On a superficial view, this objection may appear
plausible; but on reflection it is seen to be ground-

less. It does seem as if the slow process of nature
or ordinary Providence were too cold-blooded, so to
speak, for the warm temperament of Grace; as if a
Divine Love sufficiently intense to put itself to the
trouble of interposing in human affairs for the accomplishment of a beneficent design, would be unable to
restrain itself from hastening on with accelerated pace
towards fulfilment. On the hypothesis that God had
a gracious thought in His heart towards the human
race, as He is reported to have declared when He
summoned Abraham to leave his native land, how, we
are prone to ask, can we imagine him going about
the execution of his plan for the good of humanity
with such wearisome deliberation? Is the slowness
of the evolution not proof that the alleged purpose is
not a reality? But the sufficient answer to such questions is, that Grace, however willing to move quickly,
must take its rate of progress from the nature of the
work it has on hand. To speak more definitely, it
must take the recipients of benefit along with it, and
move at a pace with which they can keep up. God
does not manifest Himself in grace merely in order
to make a display, but that those to whom He manifests Himself may get the good intended for them.
Now, it is very possible for love, by too great eager-
ness to show itself in action, to defeat its own design
to bless its objects. A father, *e.g.*, in his inordinate
affection for his child, may give him all good things
at once, unable to delay till the child have reached
the years of discretion, and so in effect curse instead
of blessing his offspring. How often does it happen
in this way that children get too much of a parent's
blessing! Children, to be truly blessed, must be ed-

ucated for receiving, appreciating, and rightly using the gifts of parental love; and for this end, lapse of time, patience, waiting, is indispensable. In like manner, Divine Love, however ardent, must be content to move slowly, because men need to be trained by faith and patience and moral discipline for the inheritance of the promise. This is a familiar truth with reference to the sanctification of the individual, but it is equally true in reference to the redemption of the race; nay, is much more so, for the moral training of a race is a greatly more complicated affair than that of an individual. It takes twenty years for a child to arrive at manhood, and we ought not to wonder if it take twenty centuries for the human race to arrive at its majority, and to be prepared by the discipline to which it has been subjected all that time for appreciating the great characteristic privilege of the Christian era, that of standing in a relation of sonship to God. Nor does the long delay, though it last for millenniums, make grace cease to be grace, though it may tend to make its gracious character less obvious. Grace submitting to delay is only love consenting to be guided by wisdom. Only on the assumption that this slow method of procedure left in an unsaved state all who lived in the epoch of preparation, could its gracious character be seriously questioned. We shall see further on that such an assumption is groundless.

As little would the gracious character of the whole process of revelation be compromised, if it should appear that at certain stages in its course the actual Divine manifestations wore an aspect almost of antagonism to grace, as for example in the lawgiving.

Paul has made this thought a commonplace by his comparison of the law to the tutors and governors under which a child is placed till he arrive at his majority. The truth of the statement becomes, if possible, still clearer when we regard it in the light of our Lord's parable concerning the law of growth in the kingdom of God, as analogous to that of grain, producing first the blade, then the ear, then the full ripe corn. In the kingdom of nature growth not only involves delay which exercises the patience of the husbandman, but it proceeds by well-marked stages, all of which must be passed through ere it reach its consummation in a crop of ripe grain. And one of these stages, that of the green ear, is very unlike that of maturity. We see this more clearly in the case of fruit than in the case of grain. How unpalatable is green fruit, with its sour juices setting the teeth on edge! Yet it is a stage on the way to the mellow fruit of late autumn, whose sweet taste delights the eater. The acidity is opposed to the sweetness, yet it is a phase in the natural process of growth which has sweetness for its goal and final cause. In like manner Law may be opposed to Gospel, and yet be a phase in a revelation which has grace for its guiding idea and terminus. The law comes because it is good in its season, good for the destined recipients of blessing. For grace must accommodate itself to the needs of its object, and deal with him as he requires to be dealt with at any given time. Accommodation is an essential principle in the method of a revelation of grace. The gracious revealer, while ever keeping in view his ultimate design, must connect the particular recipient with that design in a way suited to his whole position. In accordance with this rule, after the promise came the law. There was first the beautiful blossom of the promise in the patriarchal time, then the green fruit under the law, then the ripe fruit appeared with the advent of Christ full of grace and truth. By the nature of the case the ripe fruit tarried long; for the legal discipline which was designed to prepare men for enjoying it demanded a lengthened period within which to work out its effect. During the lapse of that intermediate stage it might well seem as if God had forgotten to be gracious. But in truth He was only taking pains to insure that the ripe fruit, when it came, should have a maximum of sweetness to the human palate. The whole process from beginning to end was long, very long; but it issued in something well worth waiting for, which could not have been so good had it come much sooner, especially had it come without the intervention of the legal green ear. It was well that the blade of the promise came first, for men must know what they have to wait for, at least dimly; and in representing it as coming when it did, the Scriptures give a thoroughly credible account, for when should the blade appear if not at the beginning? Surely not when the green ear is well advanced, as those in effect say who make the promise to Abraham a mere invention of the prophets. But the promise having once been given, it was well also that men had to bear a protracted discipline of law, that they might be thoroughly weary of rules, and thoroughly drilled in the exercise of their moral senses, and on both accounts glad to welcome the day-dawn of the Gospel era bringing redemption and liberty.

The foregoing train of thought may suffice to remove objections to the method of revelation based
on the long delay which it involved before the end
aimed at was reached.   We may now, therefore, proceed to notice the objections which may be suggested
by the second feature incident to that method specified at the commencement, viz., the partiality of Divine action in the earlier stages of revelation.   The
self-revealing God proceeded by the way of *election*,
and had dealings first only with one individual, and
thereafter only with one nation.   How strange this
exclusiveness, this seeming indifference to all the rest
of the world, on the hypothesis that the purpose of
grace really concerned all mankind!   Now, there is
certainly here a superficial antinomy requiring resolution, and the resolution is to be found in a correct
conception of the idea of election and of what it involves.   Election, then, does not signify a limitation
of Divine sympathy to all intents and purposes to
the elect, or a monopoly of Divine favour enjoyed by
the latter.   The election of Abraham and of Israel
did not imply that all the rest of mankind were left
without the pale of God's gracious purpose, and
could share in none of its benefits, temporal or
eternal.   Some members of the elect race might
think it did; all of them would be tempted so to
think, for God's purpose that the Gentiles should be
fellow-heirs was hid from them, hid in God, as the
Apostle Paul says,* and they might readily mistake a
relative, temporary, and economical preference for an
absolute, eternal, and intrinsic one.   But the mystery,

---

* Eph. iii. 9.

though hid in God, was not hid from Him, nor did it remain at any time wholly dormant or inoperative in the Divine mind. The election was simply a method of procedure adopted by God in His wisdom, by which He designed to fit the few for blessing the many, one for blessing all. That being so, the apologist's task, in addressing himself to the study of the religious history of mankind, would be to inquire what a gracious purpose, having in view the whole world, but proceeding by the method of election, would lead us to expect regarding the outside nations and their religious condition, and then to consider how far the facts correspond to theoretical expectations, and how far therefore the hypothesis of a revelation of grace so conducted is historically verified. This is the attitude which it becomes the apologist, believing in such a revelation, to take up in studying the phenomena of ethnic religion. To one occupying this attitude, that study will prove a much more genial and hopeful one than it can possibly be to those who imagine that the principle of election necessarily implies, with reference to the Gentiles, absolute ignorance of God and utter exclusion from all the benefits of salvation.

It is impossible here to launch out upon such an extensive inquiry as I have just sketched ; but I may offer a few cursory remarks on the question, what the idea of revelation advocated in this volume would lead us to expect as to the religious condition of the peoples outside the pale of the chosen race. In the first place, then, from the universality of the Divine purpose, it might be confidently inferred that the heathen nations were all along the object of God's

6

benignant compassionate regard. The "mystery hid in God" must have guided the whole course of Divine Providence as the Ruler of the nations; the purpose of grace, universal in its scope, must all through the ages have influenced the Divine dealings with the children of men. It would not therefore surprise us if, in prosecuting our studies in ethnic religion, we found reason to think that God, while revealing Himself specially and systematically to the people of the election, did not altogether hide Himself from other peoples, but gave them as much light as might suffice to make the darkness of their night tolerable till the dawn should arrive; raising up now and then, here and there, men of comparatively pure, vigorous, moral sentiments, and clear religious intuitions, whose wise thoughts and worthy life should be as starlight amid the gloom of night. Nor should we think it necessary in the interests of revealed religion to disparage these prophets of paganism. On the contrary, we should gladly hail the lights of pagan religions, both because of the guidance which they gave to the peoples sitting in darkness, and likewise because of the help which they yield to ourselves, as an aid to faith in revelation. For such an aid they do really supply. To be convinced of this, we have but to ask ourselves what inference might naturally be drawn were the night of paganism absolutely unrelieved by the presence of spiritual light. Would there not then be room for doubt whether God had a purpose of grace towards the nations? How reconcile the existence of such a purpose with the total neglect of its objects, the utter abandonment of them to darkness and misery? That a beneficent being should cherish a gracious purpose, and for a time not execute it fully, is conceivable; but one would certainly expect to find the objects of the purpose treated all along in a manner that was congruous to the purpose, and conveyed hints at least of the ultimate fulfilment.

But on the other hand, the method of election having been adopted for realizing the universal design of Divine grace, we should be prepared to find traces of marked inferiority in the pagan religions as compared with the religion of the elect people. The method implies that the elect people must be subjected to a special discipline in an isolated state, in order to become eventually a source of blessing to the world; and that again implies that the people who do not get the benefit of that discipline will thereby be put at a great disadvantage, and be, in comparison to the privileged race, as a street Arab to a carefully trained boy. We should expect to find on the side of Israel, as compared with the rest of the world, traces of the advantages resulting from a carefully conducted moral and religious education. If such traces were not forthcoming, we might very legitimately doubt either the reality of the election or its utility and necessity. And it is not difficult to conjecture of what nature the traces must be. If the election was real and requisite, then it will appear on inquiry that it is very difficult for men left to their own resources to find out God, still more difficult to retain Him in their knowledge, and to live up to their knowledge, and to make steady advances in Divine knowledge. Evidences will be forthcoming that the tendency of ethnic religion is not upwards, but downwards; not to steady progress, but to degeneracy. On the other hand, a reverse tendency ought to be observable in the religion of the elect people. The path of revelation within the favoured circle ought to be as the shining light, which shineth more and more unto the perfect day. If the facts should turn out to be in accordance with these anticipations, and students of comparative religion affirm that they are, then the hypothesis of an election will be verified.

But, once more, while the fact of the election leads us to expect traces of the evil resulting from want of special religious training in the history of ethnic religion, the purpose of the election would lead us to infer that the heathen nations would not be altogether without the benefit of a Divine education. The election was meant to prepare Israel for giving to the nations the benefit of the true religion. But that preparation would be to a certain extent fruitless, unless the nations on their side were prepared for *receiving* the benefit. Therefore, just because there was an election, we may infer that there must have been a providential guidance of the world's history in all departments of human affairs, in religion, philosophy, science, art, war, commerce, meant to prepare the world for receiving and making the most of the benefit when the elect people was ready to give it. In other words, the Pauline idea of a "fulness of the time" must have its truth, not merely in reference to the Jewish people, but in reference to the world at large. As is well known, various attempts have been made in recent years to give to this magnificent apologetic idea of the Apostle a catholic scope, and to use his words as a compendious formula for the

whole religious history of mankind; the attraction
of the phrase to philosophic minds lying in this, that
it enables them to recognise the relative truth and
worth of all the great religions of the world, while
regarding Christianity as the absolute religion, the
consummation of the great process of man's religious
development. Hegel, *e. g.*, represents all the principal forms of religion as determined by the Idea of
religion, as forms which could not but appear, as appearing in no casual order, and as together constituting a process which in the time fixed by the Everlasting Reason and Wisdom of God, culminated in the
Christian religion; that is to say, the religion in which
God is perfectly manifested as Spirit, therefore the
absolute, final, perennial religion. It is a fascinating
conception of the world's religious history, and it is
not surprising that the great philosopher concludes
the introductory sketch of his " Religions-philosophie" by the remark : " This course of religion is the
true theodicy; it shows all products of the spirit,
every form of its self-knowledge, as necessary, because the spirit is living, active, and has the impulse
to pass through the whole series of its appearances to
the consciousness of itself."* A similar conception
of the world's religious history pervades the work of
Bunsen, " God in History," and the essay of Bishop
Temple on the education of the world, in " Essays
and Reviews." Bunsen regards the consciousness
which man has of God,—in one word, religion,—as
the constant motive force in the history of nations ;
and, believing as he does in a steady onward progress

---

* " Religions-philosophie," vol. i., p. 44.

in that history, he believes also in a progress in men's religious ideas from lower to higher forms, until they reach in Christianity their fulfilment. Temple conceives of the human race as "a colossal man, whose life reaches from the creation to the day of judgment," "passing through stages answering to those of any ordinary man,—childhood, youth, manhood, —and undergoing a training adapted in its course to those successive stages—in his childhood, subject to a discipline of positive rules; in his youth, delivered to the influence of models; and in full age, left to his own discretion." First come rules, then examples, then principles. First comes the law, then the Son of Man, then the gift of the Spirit. This view is a commonplace so far as it applies to the Hebrew race; the peculiarity of the essay is the application of the theory to the Gentile races. "The natural religions, —shadows projected by the spiritual light within,— were all in reality systems of law given also by God, though not given by revelation, but by the working of nature, and consequently so distorted and adulterated that in lapse of time the divine element in them had almost perished. The poetical gods of Greece, the legendary gods of Rome, the animal worship of Egypt, the sun worship of the East, all accompanied by systems of law and civil government springing from the same sources as themselves, namely, the character and temper of the several nations, were the means of educating these peoples to similar purposes in the economy of Providence to that for which the Hebrews were destined." I am not aware that any objection on the score of principle can be taken to these fine schemes. So long as the

supremacy of Christianity as the great goal to which
the history of the world was tending is recognised,
and all the other religions of the world are embraced
under the category of *preparation*, the believer in revelation may rest content. He may even receive positive gratification from speculations which tend to
confirm the true conception of revelation, as the evolution of a purpose of grace in which all mankind had
an interest. At the same time, it is well not to allow
our minds to be too much dazzled by such magnificent
generalizations, and for this purpose to remember
that they are open to a twofold criticism. In the
first place, such grand schemes look very well on pa-
per, but it may fairly be questioned whether they can
be worked out, without extensive manipulation of
historical facts. Then, secondly, the notion of preparation does not necessarily imply steady progress onwards from one degree of religious development to
another, all the stages being good in their own measure, time, and place, till the last and highest degree
is reached. We might conceive of the ethnic religions
as being a preparation for Christianity in this sense,
that they were an exhaustive list of experiments on
man's part to find out God, which were appointed to
be made that men might be thereby made ready to
welcome the light from above, through the consciousness of the fruitfulness of their own search. Paul regards the law given to Israel as a vain experiment
that had to be made, that the Jewish people might
gladly receive Christ when He came full of grace and
truth. Might not all the religions of the world be
more or less experiments of that kind? It would not
follow that there was no Providence presiding over

the world's religious history. It would only follow
that God had been for a season suffering all nations
to walk in their own ways, while not leaving Himself
without witness, but doing them good, giving them
rain from heaven and fruitful seasons, the things they
mainly sought after, filling their hearts with food and
gladness. At the same time the apologist has no interest in dogmatically asserting that the preparation
of the Gentiles for Christianity must be of this purely
negative sort. It might, we should almost expect
that it would, consist, not in mere fruitless experiments ending in despair, and in longings like those of
Plato for light from above, but also in anticipations of
truth, in ideas spiritually of kin to those of Hebrew
psalmists and prophets and sages, scattered rays of
light emanating from Him who is the Light that
lighteth every man that cometh into the world.*

If the facts of the world's religious history at all
correspond to these *à priori* inferences from the idea
of revelation, it is evident that we have no reason to
take a despairing view of the spiritual state of the
pagan nations on account of their comparative ignorance of the true God, and of His gracious will toward
men. If so, then *à fortiori* we need have no anxiety
as to the salvability of those belonging to the chosen
race who lived at the early stage of revelation, because
of a similar though not so dense ignorance. That the
knowledge possessed by such in the primitive ages
was very scanty, and the light very dim, we must admit ; to assert the contrary, is simply to deny the his-

---

* A view closely allied to this is worked out in a most interesting
manner by Dr. Matheson, in his Baird Lectures on "The Natural
Elements of Revealed Theology."

torical character of revelation. The knowledge of
God and of His will possessed by Abraham, for example, was to that of men living in the Christian era
but as the germ to the full-grown organism, or as the
acorn to the oak. He knew God as a gracious God,
but He did not know what God in His grace was going to do. Nor was such knowledge needful. It is
the knowledge of God's spirit, not the knowledge of
all that is in God's mind, that is saving. The older
dogmatists were of a different opinion, and strove to
make out for the earlier recipients of revelation a
knowledge of God's plans and purposes little less complete than that possessed by those who live in the era
of grace. This view is not only wide of the truth as
a matter of fact, but opposed to the apologetic interest of the faith, as rendering it easy for unbelievers to
raise formidable objections. Assuming that explicit
acquaintance with the scheme of salvation is necessary
to salvation, it virtually asserts that all the heathen
are lost, and that members of the elect race were saved
only by having vouchsafed to them a knowledge denied to all the rest of the world. The one assertion
lays the position of believers open to such assaults as
that of Rousseau, when he asked if it were credible
that God would confine communications necessary to
salvation to so few, and if a God who commences by
choosing one people and proscribing the rest of the
human race can be the common Father of men.* The
other assertion is open to the obvious objection that
it does not seem in accordance with the facts as recorded in Scripture. For, as Reimarus pointed out,

* *Vide* " The Confession of the Savoyard Vicar," in *Emile.*

6*

the Divine communications to Abraham did not refer to such vital matters as the Atonement and the life to come, but to much more worldly matters, such as the birth of children and the possession of a particular country. The actual history of Abraham is indeed very hard to understand on any doctrinaire theory of revelation, whether it be the old orthodox one, or such a view as that of Mr. Arnold, which makes the didactic significance of the Bible consist in the reiterated proclamation of the immense importance of righteousness. If belief in doctrines be so essential to salvation, it is hard to see why herds and flocks, sons and lands are so much more prominent than doctrines in Abraham's life. In like manner, it is hard to explain the prominence of these secularities on the assumption made by Mr. Arnold, that " Probably the life of Abraham, *the friend of God*, however imperfectly the Bible traditions by themselves convey it to us, was a decisive step forwards in the development of these ideas of righteousness."* The author of "Literature and Dogma" obviously feels that from his point of view the life of Abraham has been very unskilfully written. No wonder, for surely a writer sharing Mr. Arnold's views would have given much more prominence to Abraham's lessons in righteousness, and less to those material matters that occupy the foreground of the picture. No theory fits in to the facts as they are recorded, except that which makes revelation consist in the historical evolution of a gracious purpose, and which makes salvation depend, not on understanding what is to be the issue and out-

---

* " Literature and Dogma," p. 31.

come of the evolutionary process, but on the fact of
the gracious purpose being in God's mind. Then we
can understand the prominence given to such an apparent triviality as the birth of an heir, for that is a
necessary first step in the process of development.
Then also we can understand the scanty amount of
doctrinal instruction communicated to Abraham, such
not being indispensable to salvation. Then, once
more, we know what to say to Rousseau when he com-
plains of the proscription of the whole human race,
Israel excepted. There was no proscription in the
case: election does not mean proscription, but is a
method by which one is used to bless the many. And
God does not need to wait till the method has been
fully developed before He can do good to the many.
If His grace can reach the members of the chosen
race, though their knowledge of His purposes be small,
it can also reach those without, though their knowledge be still less. It may indeed be objected, that
on this genial and hopeful view of the compatibility
of salvation with much ignorance, knowledge seems
wholly unnecessary, and the revelation of the mystery
of grace altogether superfluous. But the objection is
easily met. In the first place, no one can rationally
pretend that the influence of God's gracious thoughts
unknown can by any possibility be equal to the influence of these thoughts known. But more especially it is to be borne in mind that gracious thoughts
never revealed are not gracious thoughts at all. It is
essential to the being of grace or love that it manifest
itself. Love unrevealed is love unreal. The time
and the manner of revelation are matters of secondary
importance, affairs of method to be determined by

love taking counsel with wisdom; but revelation on some method there must be, if there be indeed a gracious purpose hid in God's bosom.

Defective knowledge of God's gracious intentions in the early period of revelation thus appears to be by no means an insuperable objection to the method adopted in making the revelation. The difficulties, however, arising out of the moral defectiveness characteristic of the same period, may appear more serious. These difficulties present themselves to our view more or less throughout the whole Old Testament epoch, the age of preparation, and may be divided into four classes. There are those connected with the defective morality of the agents or recipients of revelation; those arising out of actions represented as being sanctioned and commanded by God; those connected with rudimentary legislation; and finally, those presented in the traces of a legal spirit in the Old Testament literature, strongly contrasting with the evangelic spirit characteristic of the New Testament. To attempt a discussion of all the topics coming under these several heads, would carry us far beyond our limits. I must therefore confine myself to a few selected points which may suffice to illustrate the bearings of the question.

Two general remarks may be premised, bearing on the whole subject. The first is, that it should not surprise us if, in the course of a Divine revelation, the morally perfect should be preceded by the morally imperfect. It is enough if the perfect do at length come, and if throughout there be a perceptible progress towards the perfect as the goal. If it should be found that such is the character of

the alleged revelation recorded in the Scriptures,—
a steady progress towards an ethical ideal eventually
realised,—we should then have no hesitation on the
score of defect in the early stages in recognising such
a reputed revelation as indeed divine. Revelation
in that case, on its ethical side, as a moral education
of the human race, would be in analogy with the
sanctification of the individual, which is not a momentary magical act, but a gradual work which
advances slowly from stage to stage till the ripe
fruit of Christian maturity at length appear. The
fact to be accentuated in connection with such a
revelation is, not the defect of preparatory stages, but
the upward progressive tendency of the movement.
The marks of its divineness are the ideal reached at
the end, and the constant advance towards the ideal.
Neither of these belongs to the order of nature. Not
the ideal; for all admit that the character of Christ
and the ethical standard set up in His teaching and
example reach a preternatural pitch of perfection.
Not the steady progress towards the ideal; for such
an advance is nowhere else exemplified, and least
of all among the Semitic races to which the people
of revelation belonged. The tendency of man, as
revealed in the history of nations, has ever been
towards moral degeneracy, both in theory and in
conduct; and this tendency, as is well known to
students, was to an exceptional extent exemplified
in the religious history of the pagan Semites. The
facts in evidence can be gathered from the pages
of the Hebrew Scriptures, as can also the proofs of
an ever-increasing purity in the moral ideas within
the pale of the chosen people; and when the two

classes of facts are placed side by side one cannot help asking the question, Whence this striking difference? The answer of faith is, that the difference is due, not to the natural genius of the Hebrew race, but to the supernatural action of God. Does it not seem a rational answer?

But can we introduce God as an agent in the moral education of Israel without compromising His perfection by making Him responsible for, or at least bringing Him into dishonouring contact with, the crude moralities of the earlier stages of the pedagogic process? The answer we give to this question will depend on the idea we form of Divine perfection; and the second observation I wish to make is, that we ought not to regard God's perfection from the Pharisaic view-point of mere majesty or negative holiness, but from the Christian view-point of gracious condescension and love. This is a reflection much needing to be laid to heart, not only by unbelievers, but also by believers in revelation. For it is the fact that the idea of God entertained by many believers is largely tinged with Pharisaism. The Divine perfection, what is God-worthy, is judged of by reference, not to the idea of *grace*, but rather to that of exaltedness above the world. The habit of so judging reveals itself variously: by *à priori* inferences as to the literary. characteristics of the Bible, viewed as a book produced by Divine authorship, not less than by the manner in which the contents of the sacred volume are interpreted. God's book must be free from everything that would be regarded as a defect in a book of merely human authorship; and if in any

part of the book a sentiment appears which seems
incompatible with God's holiness, it must be carefully
explained away. Such zealous guardianship of God's
literary and moral reputation is on a par with that
exercised by Job's friends over God's character as
the moral Governor, or by the censors of Jesus over
His dignity when they blamed Him for associating
with publicans and sinners. It is a service for which
God does not thank them, because it is in His sight
no service at all, but only a folly based on ignorance
of His character and betraying His cause into the
hands of its enemies. To all such self-elected
guardians of His holiness and majesty God says:
" Suffer Me to condescend to man's need. I am not
the Being ye take Me for. My first concern is, not
to uphold My dignity, but to communicate the blessings of My grace; and for this purpose I am willing
to stoop to whatever is necessary to bring Myself
into living connection with those whom I would
bless, so that they may indeed receive the benefit."
Only a God of whose inmost heart such words were
a true reflection would make a revelation of Himself
to man; only when we so conceive of God can we
understand, appreciate, and be benefited by the
revelation which He has actually made.

Passing now to speak of the different classes of
moral difficulties, it is easy to see the bearings of the
preceding observations concerning the Divine perfection on the supposed injury done thereto by contact with the moral crudity of the early recipients of
revelation. The objections of Reimarus on this score
were adverted to in the first Chapter; and that such
objections are not yet out of date appears from the

style in which the same topic is treated in such a
work as " The Bible for Young People." It is an
offence to the authors of this book, that the wealth
obtained by Jacob through cheating is called a blessing of God, and still more that the birthright is supposed to be conferred upon him by the Divine will,
though it was obtained at first by a disgraceful advantage taken of a thoughtless brother, and secured
afterwards by a still more disgraceful fraud practised
on an aged father. The occurrence of such gross
representations in the story of the patriarch's life is
accounted for somewhat as scholars are wont to
account for the immoralities in Greek mythology,
viz., by seeing in them traces of an early nature worship. "A nature god is not a morally good being.
And so it was possible for a man to attribute base
actions to his god and yet be religious; to be zealous
for his honour, and ready to sacrifice himself to him
if need were, and yet at the same time to be of a
very low moral type."* The character of Jacob, as
depicted in the narrative, is certainly bad enough, and
it is not our part to extenuate its baseness. In one
respect, indeed, our interest as apologists rather lies in
the opposite direction, of making the patriarch's faults
appear as glaring as possible. For the more glaring,
the more like the ancient period they belong to, the
less likely they are to be the mere invention of a
prophetic narrator, living in an age when higher ideas
of morality prevailed. The crude morality befits and
bespeaks an early time, when the process of revelation was as yet only commencing. But the question

* Vol. i., p. 247.

is, Could God have close relations with such a morally
defective person as Jacob, such a relation as is implied in his being the elected heir of the blessing?
Now, in justification of an affirmative answer to this
question, we might insist on the fact that such men
as Jacob, in spite of their defective character, are
often the objects of Providential preference, succeed-
ing in life when men of Esau-like spirit, generous,
impulsive, thoughtless, fail. And we might further
maintain that such preference was in accordance
with the dictates of moral reason, inasmuch as Jacob,
with all his grave faults, stood higher in the scale of
being than Esau, tested by the principle that every
man who exercises reflection and forethought, and
regulates his life by an aim worthy of a human
being, is superior to one who is the creature of impulse and appetite. Judged by this standard, it
might be truly alleged that Jacob, though far less
amiable, was more moral than Esau. We might say
that, granting him to be a very mean man, still he
was a *man*, while his brother was only a generous and
likable *animal*. Then we might see in the election
of Jacob, in preference to Esau, to the inheritance of
blessing, simply the Divine endorsement of this comparative estimate. And if we did adopt this view,
we should not be guilty of nature worship; that is to
say, of believing in a god who is indifferent to moral
distinctions; for the view in question does not imply either Divine approbation of Jacob's faults or
indifference to them, but simply a preference of him,
as on the whole, all things considered, the better
man—better absolutely, and better for the purpose
of the election which was to separate a people from

the rest of the world unto a high vocation. This purpose could best be served by those who were capable of appreciating the calling of God and the destiny of Israel, and it might safely be affirmed that a man like Jacob, however far below Abraham he might fall in respect to such capacity, was certainly much superior to a man of the Esau type.

There is some force, I think, in the foregoing line of thought; and yet I am not disposed to lay chief stress on it, but prefer rather to fall back on the category of *grace*, as that best fitted to help us through the difficulties of the patriarchal history. What we observe in the story of a Jacob, as in the case of any other morally defective Old Testament character, is just what we see in the Gospel records of Christ's ministry—the holy One in gracious love becoming the Friend of the sinful. In neither case was there indifference to moral evil, though in both such has been imputed by men of Pharisaic spirit. There was simply fearless contact with the morally culpable on the part of a gracious Being who had a higher end in view than merely to preserve His own holiness intact, even to make the sinful partaker of His holiness. That God had this end in view in His dealings with Jacob we ought not to doubt, any more than we doubt the motive of Jesus in going to be guest with men that were sinners. God meant to make Jacob better than He found him, and took him in hand to subject him to a moral discipline that should eventuate in a nature purified and ennobled. And the history seems to supply us with evidence that the disciplinary process reached its consummation, in that suggestive incident of the Patriarch wrestling with the angel, resulting in the change of his name from Jacob to Israel. A supplanter transformed into a Prince or Soldier of God, is a result worth taking pains for. Well might the God of grace have to do with one chargeable with grave vices of nature and faults in conduct, if the issue of His dealings was to be such a spiritual change! With such a possibility in view, we may even imagine the Divine Being selecting as the subject of His gracious influence one distinguished among his fellows, not for virtue, but for evil proclivities and habits. So Christ sought out the chief of sinners, hoping to find in them the most devoted disciples, basing His calculations on the principle: To whom much is forgiven, the same loveth much.

Of all the cases belonging to the second class of difficulties, that, viz., of questionable actions sanctioned or commanded by God, none is more perplexing on the score of justice than the wholesale destruction of the Canaanitish tribes. This instance of rude morality has, moreover, a further claim to our special attention on the ground of its peculiarly close connection with the question as to the chief end of revelation and the means adopted for its attainment. For it appears, on first view, as if in this case the end was sacrificed to the means, and the catholic purpose of grace compromised by the method of election. God, *ex hypothesi*, has it in view to bless all the nations of the earth, and He chooses a particular people to be trained for being the vehicle of blessing; and here we see Him proposing to destroy a whole group of nations to make room for the chosen race. Could the God of grace give any countenance to so

ruthless a proceeding? Could a god who was capable of such flagrant partiality cherish so humane and
benevolent intentions as we have ascribed to the
God of revelation? Is there not here some justification for the Gnostic doctrine, that the God of the
Old Testament and the God proclaimed by Jesus
Christ are entirely different beings, possessing moral
attributes utterly incompatible? That the people of
Israel did wage a war of extermination against the
Canaanites, one can easily believe, for it was the fashion of the time to conduct war in such a barbarous
manner. That they found it possible to persuade
themselves that God desired them to wage such a war,
is also easy to understand; for, as Dr. Mozley has
pointed out, the ruling ideas in those ancient ages
concerning justice were such that men could regard
as a divinely appointed duty what we now could not
believe to be our duty, though miracles were wrought
to persuade us it was. The sense of justice was then
a blind passion, which made no distinction between
the guilty and the innocent who were in any way
connected with them; therefore it would hardly
require miracles to persuade the invaders of Palestine that, if the inhabitants of the land were deserving of punishment for prevailing iniquity, they
might be devoted to indiscriminate destruction. But
the question is, How could the God of absolute
justice, and still more the God of grace, be in any
way a party to such a butchery? The question is
one to which it is not easy to return an answer completely satisfactory; but before adverse judgment is
pronounced, it is necessary to bear in mind all that
Scripture says on the subject. The Scripture repre-

sentation is to the effect that while God had destined the descendants of Abraham to inherit the land of Canaan, yet He delayed the fulfilment of the promise for this reason, among others, that the old inhabitants might not be dispossessed or destroyed before their wickedness had reached such a pitch that their destruction would be felt to be a just doom. According to the narrative in Genesis, intimation of this policy was made to Abraham himself, the Lord informing the Patriarch that his descendants should not gain possession of Canaan till four hundred years had elapsed, because the iniquity of the Amorite was not yet full. This intimation revealed the same solicitude to appear the righteous Ruler which afterwards manifested itself in connection with the destruction of Sodom. The Lord said, " Because the cry of Sodom and Gomorrah is great, and because their sin is very grievous; I will go down now, and see whether they have done altogether according to the cry of it, which is come unto Me; and if not, I will know "; and He was willing to spare Sodom if so much as ten good men were found in it. And the treatment of the two messengers in Sodom on the eve of the overthow, which was such that it were a shame even to speak of it, is carefully recorded, as if for the express purpose of preparing all readers for sympathizing with the deed of vengeance. And that story in the 19th chapter of Genesis explains what is meant by the iniquity of the Amorite. When the whole people of Canaan had become as Sodom in her fulness of bread, pride, and abundance of idleness, given up to infamous and unmentionable licentiousness, at the period of the overthrow, then her iniquity

would be full, and then it might well appear an act
of charity to humanity at large to spue her out of the
land, and to give the country to a people that would
make a better use of it.   Such is the account given
of the Divine procedure in the Book of Leviticus :
" Defile not yourselves in any of these things (unnatural vices previously mentioned), for in all these
the nations are defiled which I cast out before you :
and the land is defiled : therefore I do visit the iniquity thereof upon it, and the land itself vomiteth
out her inhabitants."   Here is no partiality of a
merely national God befriending His worshippers at
the expense of others, without regard to justice ; here,
rather, is a Power making for righteousness and
against iniquity ; yea, a Power acting with a beneficent regard to the good of humanity, burying a
putrefying carcase out of sight lest it should taint
the air.   Here is the Proprietor of the whole earth
taking a particular section of it out of the hands of
cumberers of the ground and giving it to those who
will occupy it to the general advantage ; yet acting
patiently, giving to the perverse space for repentance,
as if loath to come to extremities.   Such is the God
shown to view in this stern chapter in Israel's history ;
and it is the same picture in deed as that exhibited
in words in the familiar text : " The Lord, the Lord
God, merciful and gracious, long-suffering, and abun-
dant in goodness and truth, keeping mercy for
thousands (of generations), forgiving iniquity, transgression, and sin, and that will by no means clear :
visiting the iniquity of the fathers upon the children,
and upon the children's children, unto the third and
fourth generation."   It is the same God who at a long

subsequent time shrunk from destroying Nineveh,
because in it were six score thousand persons that
could not discern between their right hand and their
left hand, and also much cattle, while knowing full
well that when Nineveh's hour of doom came, young
and old, man and beast would be involved in indiscriminate destruction; and, just because He knew
this, shrinking long from the dread work of vengeance, dallying and procrastinating, and letting things
go fearful lengths before coming to extremities. Such
is the God of the Hebrew Scriptures throughout;
slow to wrath, yet ultimately punishing wickedness
inexorably, visiting the iniquities which have been
accumulating for generations on the head of that
generation in which sin reaches its climax; taking
far more pleasure in blessing than in cursing, visiting
the goodness of fathers upon children even to the
thousandth generation, while visiting the sin of
fathers upon children only to the fourth; so far from
being chargeable with too great proneness or haste
to punish evil-doers, that He rather often provokes
in the good (as in the case of Jonah) wonder and dis-
appointment by not calling them to account more
promptly; yet in the end executing judgment with
terrible swiftness on those who have abused His
goodness. Such is the God even of the New Testament, Christ and the apostles being witnesses; a
God most kind and good, yet capable of awful wrath
at last. Such a God Jehovah proved Himself to be
to Israel herself, not less than to Sodom and the
Canaanites. Such a God, once more, is the Power,
not ourselves, revealed in the course of all human
history. That Power puts out of the way with little

compunction degenerate and effete nations, to make
room for fresh vigorous races with stuff in them supplying material for an energetic fruitful development,
executing its notice to quit in a very rough manner.
This fact might seem to offer a sufficient apology for
the Divine action in connection with the uprooting
of the Canaanites. But Strauss insists on making a
distinction between the ordinary course of history and
God's supernatural action. The moral order of the
world has its own peculiar characteristics, and what
we have to do is not to criticise these, but to accept
them as hard facts and adapt ourselves to them.
"But when God interposes supernaturally, as all
methods of working are equally accessible to Him,
He must act in the way that is morally least objec-
tionable; therefore in the present case, having it in
view to settle the Israelites in Canaan, rather than set
on foot a war of extermination, fitted to de-humanize
the chosen people and to shock mankind, He ought
rather to have put into the mind of the original
inhabitants the impulse to emigrate to some unin-
habited part of the world, even if it were necessary to
create such an impulse."* That is to say, God ought
to have revealed to the Canaanites the existence, say,
of America, and put it into their hearts to set sail
en masse for its shores. The scheme is very humane,
and it might, if carried out, have had an important
influence on the destinies of the new world; but it is
liable to two considerable objections. The mode of
action would have been violently, magically, miraculous, unnatural as well as supernatural. Then, while

---

* "Hermann Samuel Reimarus," p. 116.

gratifying humane feeling, it would have involved a total oversight of the interests of holiness, which, even for the ultimate happiness of the world, were the supreme interests in the case. For nothing was better fitted to qualify Israel for being the vehicle of moral blessing to mankind than some terrible proofs at the beginning of her history of the Divine abhorrence of human depravity. And this remark reminds me of another consideration having an important bearing on the present topic. It is, that according to the Biblical representation the people of Israel were under the discipline of law at the time they gained possession of the promised land. This fact exercised a controlling influence on the manner of the acquisition, requiring it to be such as would serve the end of the lawgiving, the development of the sense of sin, and especially of a deep abhorrence of the two chief sins of the Canaanites, idolatry and sensuality. The same fact also involved a certain obscuration of the manifested character of God, obliging Him, as it were, to descend from the elevation of a gracious Benefactor to the lower platform of a moral Governor, dealing with Israel and surrounding peoples in accordance with the rough principles of justice revealed in the moral order of the world, which is just in tendency, and on the great scale, but to appearance unjust and indiscriminate in detail and in manifold individual instances.

It thus appears that the law, even in its ethical kernel, the Decalogue, involved for God, as the King of Israel, a certain eclipsing of His gracious character. Still more was this the case with those parts of the Mosaic law which were in themselves rude and

7

defective, such as the laws relative to marriage, divorce, retaliation, etc., and also those regulating religious ritual. I have already, in an earlier part of this chapter, indicated certain lines of thought fitted to show that the entrance of a legal phase into the process of revelation was necessary, and that the appearance of such a phase does not disannul the gracious character of revelation as a whole. What I wish now to point out is, that the rudimentary legislation, which was our third source of difficulty, while certainly concealing, did also after a fashion reveal Divine grace. In giving such laws, God was graciously accommodating Himself to the capacities of the people whose moral education He had taken in hand. The very rudeness of the legislation was a proof of Divine condescension. This important truth cannot be better put than it is in the Scriptures, especially by the prophet Hosea, by our Lord, and by the apostle Paul. The prophet, in God's name, says: " When Israel was a child, then I loved him, and called my son out of Egypt. . . . . I taught Ephraim also to go, taking them by their arms."* This is an oracle worthy of the prophet of Divine love, and sets God's action towards Israel in the early period of her history in a most gracious light. In the events connected with the Exodus, God as it were adopted an enslaved race as His son. This son it became necessary to train so that he should be worthy of his Father; and as the child was found in a very rude condition, the training could not be other than very elementary. God had to teach Israel to walk in the

* Hosea xi. 1, 3.

paths of righteousness like a nurse taking a child by the arms, and had to exercise a nurse-like condescension and patience in connection with the self-imposed task of Israel's moral education, and to become as a child Himself, speaking in broken language and giving laws of a very rude and primitive character adapted to the condition of the pupil. Paul conveys much the same idea when he describes the legal ordinances, with special reference to the Levitical ritual, as weak and poverty-stricken rudiments.* The word στοιχεία signifies literally the letters of the alphabet arranged in a row; and the idea suggested is, that the Jewish religion was fit only for the childhood of humanity, when men were, as it were, learning their letters. The figure happily conveys the truth that the rudimentary legislation and ritual of the old economy were in their time and place necessary and useful, and yet were destined to be outgrown and superseded. If, as some think, the apostle meant the figure to apply likewise to the religions of the Gentiles, then it conveys a similar truth with regard to them also. In any case the words present a very genial view of the Divine character as the moral and religious Educator of men. God appears condescending to begin at the beginning, and graciously stooping to teach the merest alphabet of morals and religion, in the hope of leading His pupils on gradually to higher things. ·

In both the foregoing representations the need for rudimentary training is shown, without imputing any blame to the subject of discipline. The pupil is

* Gal. iv. 9.

simply a child, and therefore must have such instruction as a child can receive.

In the teaching of our Lord, on the other hand, the rationale of the moral defectiveness of the Mosaic legislation is found in the morally rude condition of the subject, which He described by the expressive phrase *hardness of heart* (σκληροκαρδία). To the *sklerokardia* He ascribed the presence in the Mosaic statute book of a too indulgent law of divorce;* and to the same source He doubtless traced all other imperfect elements in the civil code of Israel, such as the barbarous law of retaliation, an eye for an eye, and a tooth for a tooth. This amounted to saying that God gave Israel statutes that were not good, because Israel herself was not good. It is a very bold thought, and yet it is a thought which had been uttered long before almost in these terms by the prophet Ezekiel.† And bold as it appears, almost to the extent of being injurious to the Divine holiness, this representation, in reality, brings the grace of God in the training of Israel more prominently into view than even the genial analogies employed by Hosea and Paul. For there is greater grace in condescending to moral perversity with a view to gradual improvement in character, than in condescending to childish ignorance and imbecility with a view to the gradual enlightenment and strengthening of the reason. Christ did not shrink from ascribing this greater grace to God; and the secret of His boldness is to be found in His own loving spirit, which shunned not contact with the sinful to such an

---

* Matt. xix. 8.   † Ezek. xx. 25.

extent as to give rise to serious misunderstanding, and earn for Him the honourable nickname of the Sinners' Friend. He understood the conduct of the Hebrew legislator through His own, and by aid thereof was able to discern grace beneath all the crudities of the Mosaic statute—grace forbearing with moral rudeness meanwhile, and steadily keeping in view a time when the *sklerokardia* should be removed, and regenerated men would be able to adopt as the law of life the ideal standard of duty.

It is evident that men could not be under a legal system capable of being characterized as it is by prophets, apostles, and our Lord, without having their whole way of thinking and feeling about God, man, and the world very seriously affected thereby. The law involved a temporary obscuration of the promise; and it was to be expected that while the obscuration lasted it should lead those who lived under it to cherish ideas concerning God and human life, duty, and destiny bearing a stamp of imperfection and demanding rectification by the light which came with the dawn of the Gospel era. This is only to say that the child's thoughts were like the discipline he lived under. It may be worth while to note in the close of this chapter, some of the chief traces of the gloom of the night to be found in the literature of the Old Covenant. The topic may belong more strictly to the Apologetic of the Scriptures than to the Apologetic of Revelation; but as the phenomena in question are among the most interesting and impressive evidences of the imperfection inseparable from the early stages of a progressive revelation, a brief reference to them cannot be considered irrelevant. In connection with the Apologetic of Scripture, the use of the study is to show that the phenomena are such as were to be expected from the method of revelation. In connection with the Apologetic of Revelation, its use is to show that the method of revelation was such as has been represented, a method involving growth and progress, and therefore imperfection in the earlier stages.

Among the phenomena which indicate the effect on men's minds of the legal discipline, may be mentioned the comparative *absence of the filial spirit* from the sacred literature of the Old Covenant, as contrasted with the New Testament. I say comparative, for I do not at all agree with those who, in ancient or modern times, have asserted that the filial spirit which regards God as a Father is entirely absent from the Old Testament. It is well known what extreme views were held by Marcion on this point ; and similar opinions have been expressed in our own day by men occupying a very different theological position from that of the Gnostic heretic. In his able work on the Fatherhood of God, the late Dr. Candlish says: "There is little or, I think I may almost say, nothing of the filial element in the recorded spiritual experiences and spiritual exercises of Old Testament believers. The Psalms entirely want it. The nearest approach to it, perhaps, is that most tenderly suggested analogy, ' Like as a father pitieth his children, so the Lord pitieth them that fear Him.' "* Surely this is an exaggeration. The word " Father " does not very often occur in the Old

---

* Lecture III.

Testament; but the filial spirit of trust in God as a gracious Being, of which the appropriate expression is the name Father, is certainly not so entirely wanting as is alleged. The child, though under tutors and governors, is not so utterly dominated by a legal spirit, as not to know whose child it is. There is not one of the Old Testament writers who does not know that God deals not with men in the strict rigour of justice, but is merciful and gracious, and that only on that ground can any one hope to stand before Him.

But while this is true, it is not less true that there is a certain obscuration of the filial consciousness discernible in the utterances of Old Testament saints,' which is due to two closely connected causes; viz., the influence of the legal covenant, and the habit of judging God's purposes by the course of outward events. The law and the theocratic conception of God connected therewith fostered in the minds of Israelites a habit of regarding God as a dealer out of rewards and punishments proportioned to men's acts. Hence, when outward events were untoward, there came a cloud between God's face and the soul of the devout man, and an inner conflict arose between two classes of thoughts, one suggested by theory on the one hand, and one suggested by a good conscience on the other: theory telling him that in unhappy circumstances he ought to regard himself as the object of Divine displeasure for his sins, a good conscience telling him that there was nothing in his conduct that could account for the frown of Providence. We see this conflict vividly represented at large in the Book of Job, and shortly in the forty-fourth Psalm.

Closely connected with the unfilial tone of Old Testament piety is the *querulousness* characteristic thereof in view of the dark mysteries of human experience. The spirit of sonship is cheerful, buoyant, optimistic; the legal spirit, on the contrary, is gloomy and desponding. Clouds of sadness and depression accordingly frequently darken the Old Testament sky. Psalmists doubt whether God be good to the righteous, seeing how bad men prosper, and good men are plagued all the day long. Prophets demand why they that deal treacherously are happy, and marvel that One believed to be too holy to regard evil with complacency, or even with indifference, should look on unmoved when the wicked devoureth the man who is more righteous than he, and suffer the innocent to be caught like fishes in the sea in the net of an Eastern despot bent on universal conquest.* This querulousness was one of the results of the legal discipline, which put the people of Israel on this footing: "Do right, and it shall be well with thee; do wrong, and it shall go ill with thee." It was a truth, but it was only a partial truth. It does go well on the whole with nations that keep God's commandments, but not uniformly or to the full extent of human wishes. It is an affair of tendency, and there are many exceptions, qualifications, and drawbacks; and over and above this the legal covenant does not exhaust the relations between God and man. These things, however, Israelites did not understand. They took the covenant as strict truth and as the whole truth, and they were therefore very much astonished

---

* Habakkuk i. 13.

to find that experience did not correspond to promise; and their feelings were embittered, and their ideas confounded, and a painful perilous spirit of doubt regarding the righteousness and the reality of Divine Providence visited their minds.

A third element in which we can trace the influence of the legal discipline in the Old Testament is what may be called the *worldliness* of its life theory. Felicity is placed largely in outward good. The method of reaching happiness is mainly outward, as that of the New Testament is mainly inward. Broadly stated, this contrast holds good; though here, as in regard to the absence of the filial spirit, we must beware of extreme statements. The conception of a felicity not dependent on external state, but consisting in inward peace of mind springing out of a faith in God not to be shaken by any untoward events, is not foreign to the Hebrew writings. Nowhere in the whole Bible does it find more beautiful and pathetic expression than in some utterances of Psalmists and Prophets. The closing portion of the seventy-third Psalm, and the concluding stanzas of Habakkuk's sublime prayer, beginning respectively with the words, " Nevertheless I am continually with Thee," and " Although the fig-tree shall not blossom," may be cited as examples. But the Psalmist and the Prophet who indited these charming lyrics did not reach the imperturbable serenity to which they give so graceful expression without a struggle. The man who at last finds in God in all circumstances a source of strength and a satisfying portion, had doubted whether God were good to Israel: and his doubt was due to his placing happiness in things without, in-

7*

stead of in God alone as the *Summum Bonum*. And
the hind-footed prophet who has at length acquired
the power of bounding securely from rock to rock
like a chamois on the Swiss mountains, is a man who
had found it hard to reconcile the holiness of God
with the seeming heartlessness of His attitude towards human affairs; and the origin of his perplexity
was the same as in the case of the Psalmist. These
men of God had both looked for happiness without
first, and only after being disappointed in that direction did they have recourse to the "method of inwardness." And the method of outwardness was that
which came natural to Israel, as we can see from
many a Psalm and from the Proverbs of Solomon.
And this habit of thought was fostered by the law
which promised material, temporal felicity as the reward of obedience to the commandments; long life
to children who reverenced their parents ; full basket
to the man that feared the Lord ; national prosperity
so long as Israel was faithful to the covenant.
" Blessed is the man that feareth the Lord, wealth
and riches shall be in his house." " Blessed is every
one that feareth the Lord; thy wife shall be as a
fruitful vine by the sides of thine house ; thy children
like olive plants round about thy table. Thou shalt
see the good of Jerusalem all the days of thy life.
Yea, thou shalt see thy children's children, and peace
upon Israel." Such are samples of the law-bred
worldliness, or, to use a less invidious expression,
" this-world-ness " of the Hebrew, in which the child
under tutors and governors appears as yet unable to
comprehend the nature of his inheritance, and looking upon the things which are seen and temporal,

not on the things which are unseen and eternal; insomuch that the hope of future glory after the tribulations of life are past, which made affliction seem
light to Paul, scarce occurred to his thoughts, and
had it been suggested as a source of consolation,
would probably only have made him melancholy.

Yet another trace of legal influence discernible
in the Old Testament may be mentioned, viz., what
we may without offence call the *vindictive spirit*.
That this is a characteristic of the Hebrew Scriptures
as compared with the teaching of Christ and the
Apostles, was recognised even by Tertullian, the great
opponent of Marcion. In his treatise " De Patientiâ,"
he speaks of that virtue as an addition to and supplement of the law, and as the only thing that had been
wanting to the doctrine of justice. " For surely they
demanded an eye for an eye and a tooth for a tooth,
for not yet was patience on earth, because faith was
not ; meanwhile, impatience was taking advantage of
the licence of the law, which was easy to be done in
the absence of the Lord of patience."* The great
Puritan theologian, Dr. Owen, expresses a similar
opinion in his treatise on the 130th Psalm. " This
duty of forgiveness is more directly and expressly
recognised in the New Testament than in the Old.
. . . . Hence we find a different frame of spirit
between them under that dispensation and those
under that of the New Testament. There are found
among them such reflections on their enemies, their
oppressors, their persecutors, and the like, as, although
they were warranted by some actings of the Spirit

---

* " De Patientiâ," cap. vi.

of God in them, yet being suited to the dispensation they were under, do no way become us, who by Jesus Christ do receive grace for grace. . . . . For all our obedience, both in matter and manner, is to be suited to the discoveries and revelation of God to us." The fact and its explanation are as represented by these distinguished doctors of theology. The spirit of forgiveness had not the same full possession of the hearts of Old Testament worthies which it attained in those who yielded themselves up to the teaching and spirit of Christ; and the cause was the habit fostered under the legal economy of regulating the life too exclusively by the law of retaliation, an eye for an eye and a tooth for a tooth, which in principle is a good law for the State, but not the highest law for the individual. The judge, if called on, is bound to give redress for wrong, but I am not bound to ask redress. I am free, in many cases, if I will, to suffer wrong; and if I be filled with the Spirit of Christ, I will often do so, and seek to overcome evil with good.

Such are some of the more salient characteristics of the literature of the ancient covenant traceable to the influence of the Mosaic legislation. It is well to understand how such phenomena are to be dealt with. On the one hand, they are to be frankly acknowledged; on the other, they ought not to be looked on as stumbling-blocks to faith, as if they were fitted to bring into doubt the reality of the revelation of grace, or the claims of writings in which such blots appear to enter as constituent parts of the record of such a revelation. For if we recognise the compatibility of the legal dispensation as a whole with a revelation of grace, as a stage in the course of its development, such recognition covers all details which can be shown to be the natural effects of the dispensation. It is inconsistent to say it was right that the law should come, that by its discipline it might prepare the heir for the promise, and at the same time to be scandalized when you find the child's thoughts taking their complexion from the system under which he lived; especially when it is considered that the direct aim of the system was, not to teach him to think imperfectly, but rather to prepare him for the era of perfection that was coming. The law was not given to make men cherish dark views of God, worldly views of life, and vindictive feelings towards those who had done them wrong. It was given to educate conscience in the sense of righteousness, and for that end it represented God as a Holy Sovereign rather than a Benignant Father, insisted on the connection between conduct and happiness in this life, and in all departments of life, and gave prominence to the duties men owe to each other, and were entitled to demand from each other. The defects in religious feeling, in the motives to good conduct, and in temper, which characterized the men who lived under the legal system, were accompanying incidents of the system, not ends which it proposed to itself. You cannot come to Mount Sinai without feeling more or less the solemn gloom and terror its environment inspires; nevertheless the people of Israel were not gathered to the Mount of Lawgiving to have their hearts filled with such emotions, but to get introduced into their life-blood the steel-drops of moral law, without which neither individuals nor nations come to much in this world.

THE FUNCTION OF MIRACLE IN REVELATION.

CHAPTER IV.

THE FUNCTION OF MIRACLE IN REVELATION.

THE chief end of miracle and prophecy, according to the traditional view handed down to us from the older school of apologists, is to supply proofs or credentials of revelation. This view is the natural accompaniment of a doctrinaire conception of revelation. Revelation, according to that conception, is the communication of a body of truths which reason could not have discovered, and to a large extent cannot even verify. Such a revelation stands in need of some evidence outside the system of doctrines claiming to be revealed, fitted to justify belief in the validity of the claim, and the consequent reception of the doctrines as given supernaturally from heaven. This need, it was to be expected, the divine Revealer would recognise and provide for. But what more satisfactory provision could be made than that supplied in biblical miracles, supernatural acts of Divine power, and in the predictive prophecies, supernatural manifestations of foreknowledge? These miracles and prophecies, therefore, are to be regarded as signs annexed to revelation to assure us that God is indeed speaking to us. This mode of viewing miracle and prophecy still holds its ground in some influential quarters. The excellent Lectures on Miracles by the late Dr. Mozley, forming the Bampton series for 1865, may be cited as a conspicuous instance of the advocacy of this view at a comparatively recent date. Dr. Mozley's mode of contemplating the subject is very clearly indicated in the following sentences from his first lecture. " There is one great purpose which divines assign to miracles, viz., the proof of a revelation. And certainly, if it was the will of God to give a revelation, there are plain and obvious reasons for asserting that miracles are necessary as the guarantee and voucher for that revelation. A revelation is, properly speaking, such only by virtue of telling us something which we could not know without it. But how do we know that that communication of what is undiscoverable by human reason is true ? Our reason cannot prove the truth of it : for it is by the supposition beyond our reason. There must be, then, some note or sign to certify to it and distinguish it, as a true communication from God, which note can be nothing else than a miracle." The author of " Supernatural Religion " adopts the same view both of revelation and of miracle, and falls back on Dr. Mozley as an authority in justification of his doing so. Christianity, the Bampton Lecturer being witness, consists of a system of inscrutable mysteries, undiscoverable by reason and incomprehensible to reason, which therefore have no self-evidencing power, but can be accredited only by miraculous deeds wrought by the agents of revelation.* The anonymous author referred to was very glad, doubtless, to have so respect-

---

* *Vide* first and following pages of the work referred to.

able authority for such a representation of revealed religion. It made his task as a destroyer comparatively easy. He had but to make such a vigorous onslaught on miracles as would suffice at least to fill the minds of readers with grave doubts and perplexities respecting the possibility and the verifiableness of the supernatural in general, in order to gain the end of unsettling conviction and detaching minds from the faith. For revelation, so conceived, has nothing in itself to commend it to men's acceptance; it is utterly devoid of self-evidencing power; its only prop is miracle, and that being knocked from under it, or rudely shaken, the whole superstructure tumbles to the ground. Yea, on such a view of revelation, the philosophical argument against miracle is likely to be reinforced by a practical argument to this effect: What is the worth of a religious system which consists of mere undiscoverable and unintelligible mysteries, which have nothing in themselves tending to produce faith, no inherent persuasive power? Is such a system worth the trouble taken to accredit it as a Divine revelation? Is it to be believed that God did take such trouble as is implied in the series of miracles wrought by Him directly or indirectly for that end? I do not suppose the author of " Supernatural Religion " meant to represent Christianity in a disadvantageous light in order to serve the purpose of controversial tactics. The probability is, that he did not know any better way of viewing the subject; and his ignorance is excusable when it is considered in what company he errs. But the fact is, that no mode of conceiving of Christianity so effectually plays into the hands of unbelief as the one in question; and the use made of it in good faith by this formidable opponent shows how important it is that apologists should take care not to state the question in such a way as gives advantage to antagonists, as I think the eminent defender of miracles has done in the passage above quoted. In the interest of faith, it is urgently incumbent on the apologist to make the relation between revelation and miracle appear more intimate and vital. The traditional view of the relation as purely external, creates an injurious prejudice against revelation, by fostering an exaggerated idea of its need of attestation. The prejudice is as unfounded as it is injurious. For, to see how different this hard outward view of Christianity, as a system of mysterious doctrines forced on our acceptance by miracles, is from that presented in the Bible, it is enough to recall to our thoughts the familiar utterance of the Apostle Paul: " This is a credible saying, and worthy of all acceptance, that Christ Jesus came into the world to save sinners."* Paul regarded this truth, which is the essence of the Gospel, as one intrinsically credible, and in itself so welcome to the sin-burdened heart, that one is not disposed to demand, or sensible of any great need for, an imposing array of miracles to compel belief in it, as if it were a thing which, without miracles, would be obstinately disbelieved, or regarded at least with sceptical incredulity. That mighty miracles were wrought by Him who came into the world, he of course believed; but he did not look on these as indispensable credentials, without which he should have regarded the fact of Christ

---

* 1 Timothy i. 15.

coming on a redemptive errand as neither credible nor acceptable. That fact, on the contrary, while not a truth discoverable by reason *à priori*, appeared to him one which, once revealed, was fitted to commend itself alike to reason, conscience, and heart ; for what more worthy of God than such compassion towards sinful, erring men? what more welcome to the burdened conscience than deliverance from the sense of guilt and the dominion of sin? what more acceptable to the heart than a sinners' friend like Jesus, who could love even unto death, and so earn as His guerdon the enthusiastic devotion of those He came to save?

Our quarrel with the traditional view of the function of miracle is, not that it is wholly false, but that it is altogether inadequate, and gives the first place to that which is secondary and subordinate, and so leads ultimately to a wrong conception of the very nature of miracle. Dr. Mozley cites sayings of Christ in proof that He admitted the inadequacy of His own mere word, and the necessity of a rational guarantee to His revelation of His own nature and commission. The texts do certainly show that our Lord referred to His own miraculous deeds as available evidence in support of His claim to be one sent from God. But they do not show that He looked on these, *viewed simply as miracles*, as the main evidence of His claims. As matter of fact He did not so regard them ; how far He was from doing this, may be learnt from His uniform answer to such as asked Him for a sign that might set their doubts at rest, which was a *refusal*. Such refusals might in some cases be accounted for by the fact that the sign-seekers were not

asking in good faith, but were merely seeking an excuse for unbelief. But in other cases, as, *e. g.*, in that
of the multitude at Capernaum, who asked, " What
dost Thou for a sign, that we may see and believe
Thee? what dost Thou work?"* this explanation
cannot be resorted to, for these sign-seekers were admirers, and in their way, for the moment, disciples of
Jesus. The reason of the refusal is to be found in
this, that the seekers of a sign wanted to see some
prodigy that stood in no intrinsic relation to Christ's
work as Saviour, but was a mere arbitrary wonder
wrought for the express purpose of accrediting the
worker, and serving no other purpose. The theory
of the sign-seekers seems to have been, that the less
moral significance a miracle possessed, the less useful
it was, the better fitted was it to serve the purpose of
evidence. To turn stones into bread, and then immediately to reconvert them into stones, had been to
them a better proof of Christ's claims to men's faith
and discipleship than the thing He had just done,
the feeding of thousands of hungry persons in the
wilderness. Such prodigies Jesus never wrought,
ever sternly refused to work; and His refusal is a
condemnation of the purely evidential view of the
function of miracles. For on that view it is in the
miraculousness of miracles that their value as evidence
lies; and this is one of the gravest objections against
the traditional theory, that it leads to a distorted and
caricaturing conception both of miracle and prophecy.
For evidential purposes, it is the thaumaturgical element in miracle and the predictive element in pro-

---

* John vi. 30.

phecy that is of chief value. Hence we find Mr.
Arnold, in the chapter of "Literature and Dogma"
which relates to the *argument from miracles*, selecting, as an imaginary typical miracle, the conversion
of a *pen into a pen-wiper*. With this typical miracle
he finds it very easy, as we shall see, to put the fool's
cap on the old English method of using miracles as
external signs wrought with a view to accredit a doctrinal revelation—a method, unfortunately, not yet
fallen into disuetude, the English mind being very
conservative and prone to keep in the beaten path.
Perhaps Mr. Arnold's chapter on Miracles will very
materially help conservative minds to arrive at the
conclusion that a way of conceiving the nature and
the function of miracle which cannot be typified by
the thaumaturgic feat of converting a pen into a pen-
wiper, is on all grounds much to be desired.

There is such a way, and it is one naturally arising
out of the view of revelation advocated in this work.
Revelation consisting in the self-manifestation of God
in human history as the God of a gracious purpose,
—the manifestation being made not merely or chiefly
by words, but very specially by deeds,—the thought
readily suggests itself that the true way of conceiving miracles, and also prophecy, is to regard them,
not as mere signs annexed to revelation for evidential
purposes, but as constitutive elements of revelation,
as forming in fact the very essence of the revelation.
Let us revert, in illustration of this statement, to the
miracles of our Lord. Christ's miraculous deeds were
all useful, morally significant, beneficent works, rising
naturally out of His vocation as Saviour, performed
in the course of His ministry in the pursuit of His

high calling, and just as naturally lying in His way, as unmiraculous healings lie in the way of any ordinary physician. In a word, Christ's miracles were simply a *part* of His ministry, and He appealed to them in evidence, not as something external added to His work as a seal,—the nature of the miracles being of no consequence, provided only they were miracles,—but as an integral portion of the work, the evidence of which was really as internal as that of His teaching, which by its intrinsic wisdom and grace came home to men's minds with persuasive force and moral authority. In perfect accord with this view is the place assigned to miracles by Jesus Himself, in His reply to the Baptist's messengers: "The blind receive their sight, and the lame walk, the lepers are cleansed, and the deaf hear, the dead are raised up, and the poor have the Gospel preached unto them."* Miracles of healing are put on a level with preaching the good tidings to those who most needed them, and their evidence is of the same kind. For the reply does not mean: Tell John that I evangelize the poor, and that I also work miscellaneous miracles as supernatural evidence of the truth of what I preach when I announce to them that I am He of whom the prophets spake, come from heaven to fulfil the hope of Israel, and to bless the sinful and miserable. It means rather: Tell John I am come full of grace in word and also in *deed*, as becomes the Anointed One of ancient prophecy. Bid him compare the facts of My ministry in both departments with the prophetic oracle beginning with the words: " The Spirit of the

---

* Matthew xi. 5.

Lord is upon Me," and then judge for himself whether prophecy and fact do not correspond.

The true view, then, of our Lord's miracles, is that they were an integral part of His ministry, and therefore of the revelation of grace made therein, not mere credentials of that ministry and revelation; that in so far as they were evidential, they were so just as His ministry in word was, and that the evidential value of all alike and altogether lay in this, that they were a revelation of God in the fulness of grace and truth. And the same observations apply in great measure to all the miracles in the Bible, those of the Old Testament not less than those of the New. A small proportion of the former were of the nature of bare signs intended to serve the purpose of accrediting God's messengers, or of aiding weak faith to believe in God's promises; but, with the exception of these, all the rest were something more than evidential appendages. The miraculous birth of Isaac was not a mere sign, it was an important step in the onward march of revelation. The plagues of Egypt were not wrought to make Israel believe that Jehovah was the true God, but to effect the deliverance of Israel out of Egypt. Their evidence was internal to revelation, not external; in them God was in the act of revealing Himself as the Deliverer. The signs in the land of Ham, and those afterwards wrought in the wilderness, were not credentials appended to some system of doctrines, but direct manifestations of a gracious mind working itself out in Providence in favour of the oppressed race of Abraham.

In view of these undeniable facts, it becomes evident how far Mr. Arnold's miracle of the change of a

8

pen into a pen-wiper is from being a fit type of the miracles recorded in Scripture. And with the true view of these miracles and their function in our minds, we can read with equanimity the words in which, under cover of a patronizing attitude of indulgence towards the ignorant multitude, Mr. Arnold treats miracles with contempt, and ridicules the use to which they are put by defenders of revealed religion. " That miracles," he says, " when fully believed, are felt by men in general to be a source of authority, it is absurd to deny. One may say, indeed : Suppose I could change the pen with which I write this into a pen-wiper, I should not thus make what I write any the truer or more convincing. That may be so in reality, but the mass of mankind feel differently. In the judgment of the mass of mankind, could I visibly and undeniably change the pen with which I write this into a pen-wiper, not only would this which I write acquire a claim to be held perfectly true and convincing, but I should even be entitled to affirm, and to be believed in affirming, propositions the most palpably at war with common fact and experience."* It is for the traditional school of apologists to answer this as best they can. I do not say that Mr. Arnold is invulnerable even from their point of view. He does, however, hit them hard, and make their argument appear in a rather ridiculous light. But as for us, the polite irony of this modern Athenian does not touch us at all. For we regard miracles as integral parts of revelation, and not as bare arbitrary signs, like the change of a pen into a pen-wiper. And we

---

* " Literature and Dogma," p. 128.

know of no miracles of that sort ; on the contrary, we regard such prodigies as the kind of miracles which the Jews desired Jesus to work, but which He resolutely refused to work. Had the miracles of Jesus been like Mr. Arnold's imaginary one, I am afraid they would not have had the effect of gaining for Him implicit credence, even in affirmations palpably at war with common fact and experience. They might indeed have won for Him a temporary popularity, but only to insure a Nemesis of ultimate contempt and oblivion, the fate which awaits all professors of thaumaturgic arts. But the miracles neither of Jesus, nor of the Bible generally, are of that sort ; and unless for the purpose of bringing into discredit the traditional mode of putting the argument from miracles, the supposition of a pen changed into a pen-wiper in connection with this topic is an irrelevance, I had almost said an impertinence.

The mode of conceiving the function of the Bible miracles has an important bearing, not only on the nature of these, but on the question as to the possibility of removing them from the Bible without materially diminishing its value for the purposes of education. This question I alluded to in the close of the first chapter, in giving an account of Mr. Arnold's views as to the chief end or use of the Bible, contenting myself with simply stating it, and reserving the discussion of it for a future opportunity. We have now come to the point at which we can with advantage consider that postponed topic. Can miracles then be, indeed, separated from the Bible without changing its character or lessening its value? Now we remember Mr. Arnold's opinion on this point,

and his confident claim to have demonstrated his
thesis, as set forth in the passage previously quoted.
He regards miracles as a blot on the Bible, which all
its admirers would wish to remove from its pages, as
one would wish to clear a friend from any stain on
his reputation. And he takes credit for having performed this service to the Bible, by demonstrating at
length that, from beginning to end, its burthen is the
supreme importance of righteousness. The preciousness of the revelation contained in the older part of
the book, the revelation made to Israel of "the immeasurable grandeur, the eternal necessity, the priceless blessing of that with which not less than three-
fourths of human life is indeed concerned—righteousness," remains the same, whether we believe the
stories about the miraculous passage through the Red
Sea and the miraculous demolition of Jericho's
mighty walls, or regard them as mere unhistorical
legends. Now, on Mr. Arnold's view of the chief end
of the Bible, his statement may be admitted to be
partially true. Grant that the Old Testament contains only the record of a so-called revelation of the
importance of righteousness, and not only the miracles named, but all other miracles become *comparatively* useless. Comparatively only, not wholly ; for
displays of Divine righteousness in miraculous judgments on evil doers and oppressors like the Egyptians,
and miracles of deliverance wrought for the oppressed,
might greatly help to deepen Israel's sense of the
truth that verily there is a Power in the world, not
ourselves, making for righteousness. I do not, however, anxiously insist on this, because I rather desire
to emphasize the previous question, viz., whether

Mr. Arnold's account of the chief end of the Bible be correct or adequate. How far miracles can or cannot be dispensed with, will largely depend on the answer to this question. Granting that to a didactic revelation of righteousness, miracles are comparatively superfluous, are they of as little consequence to a revelation of grace made by acts rather than by words—by acts of condescension, by acts revealing a special purpose, by acts forming a series knit together by the unity of a pervading plan, by acts culminating naturally in the Incarnation as the *ne-plus-ultra* of Divine condescension? No; for in that case the miracles perform an organic function in the revelation, constitute the heart and essence of the revelation. That grace cannot be manifested in any degree without miracle I do not affirm, for I admit that in the moral order of the world the rudiments of grace as well as of righteousness are recognisable. But I do say that the maximum of gracious possibility cannot be manifested without miracle, and that the more the miraculous element in the Bible is conserved, the more clearly does it appear that in that book we possess the record of a gradually unfolding gracious purpose. The more the acts by which God manifests His gracious will, stand out from the common course of nature, the more manifestly they serve the purpose intended. Take away miracle from a revelation of grace, and the revelation can hardly be known for what it is. Assume that it was merely a fancy that led Abraham to expect to become the founder of a nation destined to inherit a particular country, selected to be their home by Providence ; assume that the son through whom this dream was realised was born in the ordinary course of nature; assume that, by a lucky combination of accidents of an untoward nature, the Egyptians were made glad to be rid of their bond-slaves; assume that in all the incidents connected with the Exodus and the wilderness-life there was nothing out of the natural course, though possibly a certain amount of the unusual; assume that in the conquest of the promised land there was no power at work in favour of Israel save the power of the sword and of brave hearts;—and the consequence is, that in the whole history of the so-called chosen race, there is no clear revelation of a gracious purpose presiding over the course of events, and making all things work together for its own fulfilment. With the miracles retained as an essential part of the story, a gracious purpose towards a chosen people is indubitable; without them it is very doubtful indeed. Remove the miraculous, and what remains is only a singular combination of events, having no casual connection with each other, by which it came to pass that an Eastern sheep-owner became the father of a nation, small comparatively in numbers, but considerable in importance and notable in history. The result may create surprise, and suggest the thought of some controlling influence at work, shaping events so that they might have this issue. But it is not more surprising than the products of nature, which exhibit in a wonderful degree an aspect of design suggesting a Designer, but not stringently proving it so as to exclude the contrary opinion. Retain the miracles, and the gracious purpose is stringently proved, and the contrary opinion excluded as untenable. The miracles and the purpose thus stand or

fall together. To certify, beyond all doubt, a gracious purpose, miracle is necessary. I do not say, I
do not need to say, that all the remarkable events
connected with Israel's history were in the strict sense
miraculous. Given as much of miracle as makes evident the fact of a gracious purpose, then we can afford
to admit that this or that link in the chain of events
whereby the purpose was fulfilled was not supernatural, save in the intentional use of it for such fulfilment, because God can and does work out His purposes by ordinary as well as by extraordinary Providence. But unless some part of His working be
supernatural, it is always possible to deny that conscious Divine purpose and a living gracious Providence
are revealed in human affairs. The only thing verifiable is a neuter Power, or blind tendency working
retributively for righteousness, or electively for the
benefit of favoured individuals or races.

The need for miracle to overcome doubt, becomes
still more apparent when the moral condition of man
is taken into account. The sin which creates the necessity for a revelation of grace, also makes the recipient of revelation indisposed to believe that the
Divine thoughts towards him are thoughts of peace,
unobservant of the traces of grace in nature and Providence, therefore slow to understand the loving-kind-
ness of the Lord. An evil conscience is sceptical concerning Divine benignity, prone to fear and apprehen-
sive of the worst, ready enough to recognise the traces
of the Judge, backward to discern the countenance
of the Father. The trusting spirit which rests in the
truth of the Divine Fatherliness has first to be created;
there is an antecedent distrust to be subdued by a

special display of love so signal as to render unbelief, on the part even of the most faithless, all but impossible. This special display we discover in the miraculous deeds of God recorded in the Bible. These deeds God wrought to make His grace manifest and undeniable to sinful men ; and not otherwise, as Rothe has well remarked, could He have made it manifest to such recipients of His favour.

In full accordance with these views as to the necessity of miracle in connection with a revelation of grace, are the representations of Scripture. A marked emphasis is laid by the Bible writers,—psalmists and prophets, —on the marvellousness of God's works, in connection with thanksgivings for His grace. " Remember His marvellous works that He hath done ; His wonders and the judgments of His mouth." The wonders referred to are those wrought in the land of Ham ; and the psalmist accordingly closes his song of praise by declaring these wonders to be a fulfilment of God's gracious purpose and promise. " For He remembered His holy promise, and Abraham His servant. And He brought forth His people with joy, and His chosen with gladness : and gave them the lands of the heathen : and they inherited the labour of the people ; that they might observe His statutes, and keep His laws."*

Still more remarkable is the emphasis laid on the miraculous power of God by the unknown Prophet of the Exile. Having in his view the second great manifestation of God's redeeming grace towards Israel, the deliverance from captivity in Babylon, the prophet

---

* Psalm cv.

claims for the Divine Redeemer, in the most absolute
manner, a power of miraculous initiative. The God
of this new deliverance needs to be, and accordingly
in the prophetic idea He is, one capable of doing new
things. Not only so: He is capable of doing new
things in new ways. The prophet claims for God a
twofold originality: not only in the matter, but also
in the manner of His wondrous works. Whereas of
old the miracle consisted in making a way through
the sea, the new miracle is to consist in an achievement of an opposite kind, viz., in making a way in the
wilderness, and rivers in the desert.* It is a poetical
representation, doubtless, but it is more, even the
pregnant suggestion of the deep philosophical truth,
that the God of grace is utterly exempt from bondage
either to the fixed course of nature, or to the past
course of history. He is not obliged in His action to
keep within the groove of natural law, or to conform
to ancient precedent. His power was not exhausted
in the first creation, nor His invention in the means
by which in former times He accomplished His ends.
There is no limit to His power, no limit to His capacity for new ideas. " He fainteth not, neither is weary,
and there is no searching of His understanding."†
Surely a most worthy conception of God, superior far
to that cherished either by philosophic naturalism or
by theological conservatism, one of which denies to
God the power of doing absolutely new things, and
the other, while ascribing to God miraculous power,
virtually denies to Him the power of doing new things
in new ways, and makes Him the slave of old modes

* Isaiah xliii. 18, 19.   † Isaiah xl. 28.

8*

of action, obliged to repeat Himself, and debarred by venerable custom from every form of activity that wears the aspect of innovation. The prophetic conception is the most congenial to the revelation of grace; and wherever strong faith in such a revelation,—faith worthy to be called *evangelical*,—prevails, this conception of God will be welcome. Witness Christ Himself, who thought it no reproach to His Gospel that it was novel—a new wine and a new garment; and Paul, who, with obvious reference to the prophetic oracle above alluded to, claimed it as a mark of the Divine origin of Christianity, that it made all things new.*

It thus appears that miracle cannot be separated from the Old Testament without changing its character and lessening its value. In removing the miraculous, you change the fact-basis from which your idea of the chief end of revelation is formed. The Hebrew Bible, as the record of a so-called revelation, may still remain a very excellent book; and it may be a very good service rendered to society in these sceptical times, to show how much edifying matter remains after the *Zeitgeist* has expurgated from the old book all that it does not relish. All I mean to say is, that the Hebrew Bible is quite a different sort of book after the process of expurgation; and the revelation of which it is the record is of an altogether altered, and may I not say much inferior, character. And if this be true of the Hebrew Bible, it is if possible still more emphatically true of the New Testament. Mr. Arnold thinks he can accomplish the feat

* 2 Cor. v. 17.

of purging the New Testament of miracle without
detriment to its intrinsic worth, by treating the
miraculous narratives, with exception of the healing
miracles (which are deemed capable of being reduced
to natural events by means of the as yet little studied
science of *Moral Therapeutics**), as legendary tales
due to the pious credulity and miracle-mongering
spirit of the honest but often mistaken reporters, and
by laying stress on those gospel sayings which, with
his critical acumen, he can certify to be the genuine
logia of Jesus. The essence of Christ's religion is
quite independent of miracles, for it consists in these
two things: a method of attaining the reward of
righteousness, and a secret; the method, inwardness,
the secret self-denial. Now here, again, a part, and
not the most important part, is taken for the whole.
That Christ did teach the ethical doctrines Mr.
Arnold ascribes to Him has been already admitted.
But the proclamation of these truths, as I have also
already pointed out, was not the whole of His mission. Whether we take the Synoptists, or Mr.
Arnold's favourite Evangelist, the author of the
fourth gospel, as our authority, we must come to
this conclusion. The Synoptists put into Christ's
mouth what the keenest critical acumen must recognise as a genuine saying, oft-repeated it would seem,
" the Son of Man came to save the lost." John, in
the prologue of his gospel, says: " the Word was
made flesh and dwelt among us full of grace and

---

* On this favourite device of modern naturalism, to enable it to
recognise the historical character of the Gospel record without doing violence to its philosophy, *vide* my work on the " Humiliation
of Christ," second edition, Lecture V.

truth." The foremost idea of all the evangelists is,
" Jesus Christ a manifestation, in its fulness, of Divine
grace." Now the question is: Can you separate
the miraculous from the gospels, and retain this as
the leading idea of Christ's ministry—Divine grace
revealed in fulness? No: the Incarnation itself is
involved in the idea; for if the Incarnation is not
true, then the revelation of grace falls short of what
we can conceive it to be. And how congruous to the
idea of God become flesh and dwelling among men
full of grace that forth-flowing of Divine power in
all directions to beneficent effects, to which Jesus appealed in proof that He was Christ! Without these
miracles,—for so I must continue to regard them,
with all due deference to "moral therapeutics,"—
Jesus had been a living contradiction; full of grace as
a copious gushing spring, yet a well without water.
He must do miracles, not in order to prove formally
that He is what He claims to be, but to be consistent
with Himself, true to Himself, like Himself. What
can the spring do but flow? and what should Incarnate Grace do but *be* gracious, according to the
measure of His power, doing good in every possible
way as one full of the enthusiasm of humanity?

To this, however, it may be replied: Yes, in every
possible way; but the question is, What ways are
possible? Must not physical miracles be excluded
as impossible? Even after they are excluded, are
there not left in the gospel narratives materials for
constructing the idea of a very gracious Saviour, at
once able and willing to help us in our manifold
infirmities? Have we not still a perfectly holy and a
perfectly loving being, who, both by His holiness and

by His love can lay hold of the sinful and lift them
out of their degradation into a very heaven of peace
and purity? Such in effect is the Christ recently
offered to our faith and worship by Dr. Abbott with
an earnestness of conviction deserving of our highest
respect.* But whether we can rationally or permanently rest in such a Christ, is another question. A
Christ perfectly loving, who does no miracles such as
those recorded in the Gospels, is certainly no contradiction, if miracles are impossible; for love cannot
be expected to work impossibilities. But is a Christ
perfectly *sinless*, yet incapable of physical miracles,
not a contradiction? The only legitimate ground
for the assertion that Christ could not work physical
miracles, is that taken up by philosophic naturalism—that the miraculous in every form is impossible. But is not a sinless being a miracle, not less
really that it is a miracle in the moral instead of
in the physical sphere? It is so regarded by all
naturalistic theologians, such as Keim, who accordingly does not hesitate to ascribe to Jesus moral
defects, while fully acknowledging His general excellence. Unquestionably this is the philosophically
consistent view to which all deniers of the miraculous
must ultimately come. The alternatives we have to
choose from, therefore, are: a Christ miraculous in
His person, character, and work; or a Christ miraculous in none of these respects, not even in respect of
character, but at most only a remarkably good, wise,
and humane man. Such a man is doubtless something to be thankful for; but he is hardly what

* *Vide* " Oxford Sermons "; also, " Through Nature to Christ."

humanity needs for its Saviour and Lord. He who is to occupy that high position must be divine and sinless; and none who with full intelligence see in Christ the Wonderful in these two respects, can long hesitate as to the other elements of wonder. It does indeed take some courage in these scientific times to continue to believe in the Gospel miracles, however historical the narratives may appear; and it requires, perhaps, more courage still to hold fast the oldfashioned faith unabashed by the grand oracular manner in which Mr. Arnold, inspired by the *Zeitgeist*, settles the vexed question of miracles by a wave of the hand so to speak, or, to speak literally, by a single quotation from Shakspeare. "It is," says the apostle of modern culture, "what we call the time-spirit that is sapping the proof from miracles; it is the *Zeitgeist* itself. Whether we attack them or whether we defend them does not much matter; the human mind, as its experience widens, is turning away from them."* If this be indeed so, then to continue believing in miracles is to run the risk of being voted a Philistine, and to defend one's opinion is a waste of time. But for our comfort let us remember that the *Zeitgeist* is a sprite of changeable humour, and that the faith in miracle has been again and again discarded as out of date, and taken up again as faith in Divine grace revived; a fact corroborative of our instinctive conviction that miracles and a revelation of grace go together.

But at this point we are reminded of the *dictum* of Spinoza, that miracles, far from revealing the highest

* "Literature and Dogma," p. 129.

truth concerning God, do not reveal even the lowest
and most elementary, not even the fact that God exists: the proof being, that if miracles mean events
whose causes are unknown, they are simply things
incomprehensible, therefore things from which we can
learn nothing; and if they mean events contrary to
nature, they tend rather to breed scepticism as to the
Divine existence than faith in God, inasmuch as what
is contrary to nature is contrary to the first notions
on which our belief in the existence of God is based.*
Now, as Dr. Mozley has pointed out, Spinoza regards
a miracle as a mere marvel, beginning and ending
with itself. And it cannot be denied that when so
regarded a miracle is an event to which no significance
can be attached. The only effect of an isolated
prodigy, is to make beholders stare. But it is altogether otherwise with a miracle viewed in relation to
other events which tend to give it meaning, say, such
a miracle as the healing of the blind man, taken in
connection with a previous intimation given by Christ
of an intention to restore to him his sight. Dr.
Mozley remarks, that " the evidential function of a
miracle is based upon the common argument of design as proved by coincidence. The greatest marvel
or interruption of the order of nature occurring by
itself, as the very consequence of being connected
with nothing, proves nothing; but if it takes place in
connection with the word or act of a person, that coincidence proves design in the marvel and makes it a
miracle; and if that person professes to report a
message or revelation from heaven, the coincidence,

* *Vide* chapter i p. 37.

again, of the miracle with the professed message from God, proves design on the part of God to warrant or authorize the message. The mode in which a miracle acts as evidence, is thus exactly the same in which any extraordinary coincidence acts: it rests upon the general argument of design, though the particular design is special and appropriate to the miracle." * This passage explains how a miracle may reveal something of God, even when regarded as a sign expressly wrought for an evidential purpose. Even an arbitrary miracle like that supposed by Mr. Arnold, by being previously fixed on and preannounced as to be wrought for the purpose of accrediting a divine messenger, would thereby cease to be a mere prodigy, and become a revelation of Divine thought. But the value of miracles as sources of knowledge concerning God, is greatly enhanced when they are regarded, not as signs attached to, but as integral parts of a revelation, and further, not as isolated displays of power, but as interdependent members of a great organism of revelation in which a Divine purpose is immanent throughout. Suppose that the miracles of Christ had been mainly of the nature of prodigies wrought for the avowed and preannounced purpose of substantiating His claims. In that case they would of themselves reveal nothing concerning the worker except that He was in possession of very remarkable power, and that He wished to be taken and might reasonably be taken for what He claimed to be. But the actual fact is, that Christ's miracles were direct revelations of Himself, revelations of the

* "Bampton Lectures," p. 24.

inmost thoughts of His heart, insomuch that in their absence we should with difficulty believe Him to be what He claimed to be; not for the reason given by Dr. Mozley, that to proclaim Himself God's eternal Son, the Saviour of the world and the head of the Divine kingdom, without substantiating His claims by miracles, would indicate madness or insanity; but because in that case, as already indicated, He would be in contradiction to Himself, and present the spectacle of a character assumed, but not sustained or played out. On the other hand, with the recorded miracles as an integral portion of His history, we feel that Christ presents to our view a thoroughly consistent harmonious character, in which every feature we looked for is fully developed, and all bear out the title, "God manifest in the flesh in the fulness of grace."

The true key to the Spinozan doctrine as to the valuelessness of miracles for the purpose of revealing God is a speculative conception of the universe which excludes miracle as impossible. Miracles can prove nothing only to those to whom they themselves cannot be proved. Every man who believes in miracles as matters of fact sees in them this much at least : a supernatural power or will at work. A miracle believed in as an actual occurrence, reveals the presence of a non-natural causality; that is to say, of a will ; for will is the only supernatural power with which we are acquainted. Men of a sceptical temper, however, will hardly be persuaded that a miracle in the strict sense, *i.e.*, an event which could not have had a natural cause, has occurred. We could conceive such men witnessing some of the miraculous events in our

Lord's life, and finding themselves unable to deny the
" sensible fact," and unable to account for it ; yet
hesitating to draw the inference that it had a supernatural cause, and contenting themselves with regarding it as an inexplicable phenomenon. This is, indeed, the position taken up by Baden Powell, in his
essay on miracles, in " Essays and Reviews." His
thesis is that no testimony can reach to the supernatural, or prove more than that something extraordinary
and perhaps unaccountable has taken place. That it
is due to supernatural causes is entirely dependent on
the previous belief or assumption of the parties. This
dogma either amounts to the truism that the senses
do not actually perceive the supernatural cause, but
only supply material for a rational inference as to the
presence of such causes, or it signifies that no testimony can establish a fact for which no other than a
supernatural explanation can be suggested. That the
writer referred to had the latter thought in his mind
is clear from these words : " The proposition that an
event may be so incredible intrinsically as to set aside
any degree of testimony, in no way applies to or af-
fects the honesty or veracity of that testimony, or the
reality of the impressions on the minds of the witnesses, so far as it relates to the matter of sensible fact
simply. It merely means this, that from the nature
of our antecedent convictions the probability of some
kind of mistake or deception somewhere, though we
know not where, is greater than the probability of the
event really happening in the way, and from the
causes, assigned." In other words, two doors are
open to the sceptic who wishes to escape from the
supernatural. The one, This fact admitted to be

such as witnessed or reported, may have had a natural cause; the other, This fact for which as witnessed or reported no natural cause can be conceived, may not have happened as it appears, or has been reported. The senses of witnesses may have been deceived. For one who is resolved always to make his escape from faith in miracles by one or other of these doors, the *dictum* that testimony cannot reach to the supernatural really means there is no supernatural to be reached. On the other hand, when the supernatural is regarded as real and accessible, miracles will be considered at least possible. It will not be assumed that escape may always be effected by one or other of the doors indicated. There may still, of course, be a very praiseworthy desire to verify the miraculous fact. But a fact of the kind will be deemed verifiable, and when verified it will be held to be evidence of a supernatural cause or will at work.

This, however, does not amount to much in the way of revelation, especially when it is considered that according to the Bible doctrine, miracles may be wrought not merely by the will of God, but also by other supernatural agents, not even obedient to God, but acting contrary to the interests of His kingdom. It has been thought by opponents of revelation that this fact is fatal to the evidential function of miracles. This, however, is too sweeping an inference. The fact merely shows that some consideration of miraculous manifestations is necessary in order to eliminate doubt as to the character and purpose of the Being who is at work. This is certainly the case. The mere fact that a supernatural power has been displayed does not of itself indicate with whom I have to do. It simply shows that I am in contact with a higher will of some kind, good or evil. Whether good or evil, remains to be determined by the nature of the transactions. I learn with whom I have to do in miraculous acts, just as I learn with what manner of persons I have to do in my intercourse with my fellow-men. Here the law applies : " by their fruits ye shall know them." Christ appealed to that law in connection with His own miracles. " If I cast out devils by the spirit of God, then the kingdom of God is come unto you." It will be seen that this sort of evidence is cumulative in its effect. The revelation of the moral character of the higher will that is at work is made gradually; it becomes clear as the number of acts are multiplied, and as their mutual connection becomes apparent, evincing the existence of a purpose indicative of a certain mind. It is thus we come to know the moral character of human wills ; it is just in the same way we come to know the character of a super-human will. One act of miraculous power suffices to reveal the presence of a higher will, and to start the enquiry, what sort of a will is this which I see work-ing ? It is possible that the very first act may reveal the nature of the will, just as there are single actions performed by men which leave us in little doubt as to what manner of men they are. But in connection with acts performed by supernatural agency, it is natural that we should be slower in coming to a con-clusion, and need a number of acts, all of kindred import, to reveal the moral character of the source of power. Such seems to have been the case of Christ's disciples. They believed in Him after a fashion on the very first display of miraculous power ; but their first faith was provisional and stood in need of confirmation. And it received the confirmation which it needed, from every new exercise of miraculous power by their Master, until at length it was established beyond the possibility of being shaken, so that even when their now well-known Leader spoke in a way which shocked hearers and sent multitudes of lightly attached disciples away in disgust, they could calmly abide with Him and say: "We believe and are sure that Thou art the Holy One of God."* In a similar way was the faith of Israel in Jehovah established. When Israel's God began that course of action which had for its aim and issue the Exodus, the question was raised : Who is this that is showing Himself to us ? Moses told them at the outset : " I Am hath sent me unto you." That was, so to speak, the hypothesis to be verified inductively by subsequent events. By the time they got to the farther shore of the Red Sea, the emancipated slaves could have little doubt that a friendly divinity had been at work on their behalf, and were prepared to sing. the song of triumph led by Miriam :

> " The Lord is my strength and song, and He is become my salvation,
> He is my God, and I will prepare Him an habitation,
> My father's God, and I will exalt Him."

The sympathy with the oppressed against the oppressor, displayed in the whole course of the Exodus, revealed a beneficent Being. The wonders wrought in the land of Ham revealed a mighty Being. The

* John vi. 70.

overthrow of the Egyptian host and of Egypt's great king, and the contempt poured on Egypt's gods by the demonstration of their impotence, showed the beneficent higher power to be the King of kings and God of gods.

These examples suggest the thought that the knowledge of God through His extraordinary Providence, is reached in the same way as the knowledge of God through His ordinary Providence. All theists believe that we may competently attempt to learn something concerning God from nature and from history. Some even who are not theists admit that we may form from the same sources some conclusions regarding the existence of a moral order of the world. And all, theists and non-theists, admit that the knowledge thus acquired is the result of an inductive process. A single event in Providence or history may be of very dubious significance; many isolated events are of very indeterminate character, leaving room for the question: Is God indeed good to Israel, does He really care for the right; is He not rather a Being to whom right and wrong, good and evil, are matters of indifference, so far removed from the world that such distinctions are invisible to His eye? But when a large and a connected view of history is taken it becomes apparent to the enquirer that there is indeed a God that doeth righteousness, "a Power, not ourselves, making for righteousness." Just so is the character of God read off from the phenomena of extraordinary or miraculous Providence. Isolated miracles, like isolated events in the ordinary course of history, may leave it doubtful who or what manner of being the agent is; but the doubt is elimi-

nated as the series of miraculous acts lengthens, and
the purpose by which the whole series is pervaded
becomes increasingly clear, till at length the beneficent power who has been at work is openly and
fully revealed. It would be hard for Abraham to
recognise the suggestion to sacrifice Isaac as a voice
coming from a God who was his gracious Benefactor.
It would need a second voice, rescuing at the last
moment the destined victim, to indicate the source
of the first. But taken altogether the Divine acts of
self-manifestation to the patriarch could leave no
doubt on the mind of the latter that the Being with
whom he had to do was his Friend. God's dealings
with Abraham, on review, could not but appear luminous with a gracious purpose. In like manner one
or two isolated miracles out of the whole number of
wondrous works wrought by Christ might excusably
puzzle the beholder. But no candid mind surveying
the whole series could have made the suggestion that
these miracles were wrought by the power of Satan
or any of his servants. Celsus can hardly have been
in earnest when he insinuated that the miracles of
the gospel were like the tricks of magicians. At all
events, by making the suggestion he gave his Christian opponent the opportunity of offering a very
complete and crushing reply. " Show me," said
Origen, " the magician who calls upon the spectators
of his prodigies to reform their life, or who teaches
his admirers the fear of God, and seeks to persuade
them to act as those who must appear before Him
as their judge. The magicians do nothing of the
sort, either because they are incapable of it, or because they have no such desire. Themselves charged

with crimes the most shameful and infamous, how should they attempt the reformation of the morals of others? The miracles of Christ, on the contrary, all bear the impress of His own holiness, and He ever uses them as the means of winning to the cause of goodness and truth those who witnessed them. Thus He presented His own life as the perfect model, not only to His immediate disciples, but to all men. If such was the life of Jesus, how can He be compared to mere charlatans, and why may we not believe that He was indeed God manifested in the flesh, for the salvation of our race?"*

In the foregoing observations I have virtually disposed of a problem which, in the older apologetic treatises, is thus formulated: Do the miracles prove the doctrine, or does the doctrine prove the miracles? The question arises out of the fact that in the Scripture it is contemplated as a possible case that miracles might be wrought by agents of evil bias, and showing their evil bias by teaching false doctrine. It is a question which concerns those who regard miracles chiefly as evidential signs, attached externally to a doctrinal revelation, much more nearly than those who look on miracles not as mere signs, but as sources of doctrine. The problem, however, remains for them also, but in an altered form. For them doctrine and miracles go together as manifestations of character or purpose, like the words and deeds, faith and life, of an ordinary human agent. In all manifestations of character, whether by word or by deed,

---

* Origen, "Contra Celsum," i. 68. Pressensé, "Martyrs and Apologists," pp. 619-20.

in the case of ordinary agents, or in the case of extraordinary, there may be an element of ambiguity, and the problem is to show how that element of ambiguity is to be eliminated, so that the character, spirit, and purposes of the agent may be certainly known. And our answer is, that the ambiguity is gradually eliminated as the mind of the agent unfolds itself in action. Whether the actions through which character is revealed be natural or supernatural, makes no difference.

This being so, it will be at once apparent what an advantage it must be to be placed in a position whence it is possible to survey the whole series of acts whereby God manifested Himself to the world as the God of grace. This is our case, and being so placed we are in some respects more favoured than the first recipients of revelation, who had the opportunity of witnessing some of God's wondrous works. Our first impression, probably, is that we who live in an age so far removed from the years of the right hand of the Most High, are at a great disadvantage as believers in revelation compared to those to whom God manifested Himself directly as the Revealer. We fancy that they had in it their power to be much surer that a revelation was actually being made than we can be that a revelation has been made. But this is to a large extent a delusion. The evidence to us that a revelation has been given is the character of the revelation viewed as a whole, including miracles and prophecies as part and parcel thereof. To a theist it is intrinsically credible that the living loving God in whom he believes will reveal Himself in history, in the fulness of His grace. He does not pre-

9

tend to demonstrate *à priori* that God must do so, but with his conception of God he will not be incredulous as to the fact of His having done so; and, if on a conjunct view of the alleged revelation in its whole lengthened course, he find the self-manifestation of God in grace God-worthy, he will accept the revelation as a veritable one, until very cogent reasons have been adduced why he should not. Now this is the actual state of the case. The alleged revelation, as it lies before us recorded in the Book, is God-worthy. And as it lies there, a completed revelation, we are in a position to feel the force of the internal evidence arising out of its God-worthiness, with far more effect than the first recipients. They had the advantage of being eye-witnesses of God's miraculous self-manifestation as the omnipotent, omniscient One; in regard to that we are dependent on their testimony, and on the historical record, which cannot produce as great a degree of certainty as seeing for one's self yields. But, on the other hand, we have the compensating advantage that the completed drama of revelation is before our eye, revealing in all its moral sublimity the gracious condescension of the Most High, stooping down to the level of His sinful creatures, "to revive the spirit of the humble, and to revive the heart of the contrite ones." And the result is that, unless our conception of God be such as to render that drama of grace impossible, the sublime spectacle produces conviction, and we take the whole to be what it gives itself out for, a veritable supernatural Revelation. We, in the end of days, when the long process of evolution is complete, far removed from the time when God made Himself known to the fathers, are, compared to them, like men who contemplate the whole *cosmos* as an evidence of a Divine Designer, compared to persons whose attention is engrossed by a single striking instance of design. The men of revelation had under their eye single instances of Divine grace revealed in miracles and prophecies, or, at most, a limited number of instances. We, on the other hand, have before our eye a complete system of Divine self-manifestations, spread over thousands of years, made to many different individuals; and observing the harmony which pervades the whole, and the gracious mind that gives unity to the long series, we feel as strongly convinced that we have here God manifesting Himself in grace, as in contemplating the *cosmos* of nature we feel assured that therein is revealed a wise and beneficent Maker and Preserver of all.

In the whole of the preceding discussion we have been regarding miracles as something more and higher than evidential signs of a doctrinal revelation; as constituting, not merely proving, a revelation. It may be well in conclusion to remark, though it scarcely needs to be formally pointed out, that miracles may imply much more about God than they expressly reveal, and may sustain, as the foundation of a doctrinal edifice, much more than they contain. Besides revealing a positive purpose of grace, they may teach, by implication, essential truth concerning the nature of God, *e.g.*, the doctrine of His Personality. This statement will be illustrated and vindicated more fully when we come to consider the *doctrinal significance of revelation;* meantime I take occasion to refer to an objection brought by Lessing to the competency of miracles to reveal or justify belief in eternal truth. In a tractate on "*The Demonstration of Spirit and of Power*," the demonstration of spirit meaning prophecy, and the demonstration of power, miracles, he maintains the thesis, that history, even miraculous history, can never be the basis of faith in eternal truth. Without calling in question the historical value of the sacred writings, he affirms that as no historical truth can be demonstrated, so nothing can be demonstrated through historical truths. That is, he goes on to say, in large capitals, as if the statement were of vast moment, accidental historical truths can never be the demonstration of necessary truths of reason. The real drift of this famous dictum is that revelation is of very little importance, because through such a revelation as we have in Scripture we could not be sure of anything being true unless we had other means of attaining unto certainty, viz., reason. The only function left to revelation on this view is that of suggesting thoughts to be afterwards verified by reason. The position laid down with such oracular confidence is thoroughly characteristic of the eighteenth century, and specially of the Aufkläring period, whether we have regard to the conception of revelation as having for its aim to put in circulation abstract ideas, or to the mean estimate implied therein of the value of history. It might be sufficient to say in the way of reply that the end of revelation is not merely or chiefly to put in circulation ideas of reason, but to reveal God Himself in an aspect which the human mind can recognise as God-worthy, but which it could not without revelation be sure of; not merely be-

cause the truth revealed is so majestic we hardly dare
to entertain it, but also because that truth without
revelation by action would not be true, inasmuch as
grace which is never manifested in deeds, is no grace
at all. Not that we hold God bound to manifest
Himself in grace; we recognise fully the Divine freedom and sovereignty. Nevertheless, God being what
we know Him to be, the manifestation of Himself in
grace, given the fact of sin, might be said to be a
matter of course; and equally a matter of course
might we regard the self-manifestation of God as
Fatherly love irrespective of the fact of sin; such a
revelation being to a sinless world what a revelation
of grace is to a sinful world.* The truth that God
is love is not a necessary truth like the truths of
mathematics, nor a merely accidental truth like the
historical fact of the invasion of Britain by Julius
Cæsar. It resembles rather the truths of physical
science, such as the law of gravitation or the compo-
sition of light, truths for the discovery of which observation is necessary, yet truths which once ascertained are as certain as any proposition in Euclid,
though not in the strict sense necessary truths.

Such is the nature of the truth expressly revealed
by miracle and prophecy, viz., the Divine purpose of
grace. But I have said that truths of an essential or
necessary character, such as the Divine Personality,
may be implied in a miracle-revelation; it is therefore needful to consider the question raised by Lessing, how far historical miraculous facts can avail to
sustain faith in such truths. Lessing argues thus.

---

* So Schweitzer.

Suppose I have nothing to object to the statement that Christ raised a dead man, must I therefore hold it as true that God has a Son, His equal in essence? If I have no objection to make to the historical truth of the statement that Christ Himself rose from the dead, must I therefore regard this risen one as the Son of God? That Christ, against whose resurrection I can offer no historical objections of weight, gave Himself out on account of His resurrection as the Son of God, and that His disciples on that account held Him to be such, I heartily believe. But now with these historical truths to spring into an entirely different class of truths, and to desire of me that I should alter all my metaphysical and moral ideas in conformity therewith; to suggest to me that I must change all my fundamental ideas of the essence of God—if that is not a μετάβασις εἰς ἄλλο γένος, I do not know what Aristotle meant by the expression.* To this attempt to rob historical facts of all moral and theological significance it is enough to reply, that what Lessing objects to in his own case, as an unreasonable demand, has been realized in thousands of instances. Facts believed changing men's whole way of thinking about God, and man, and the world, and their relations to each other, their whole theory of the universe, in short, is not so rare a phenomenon that philosophers should hold up their hands in astonishment at the very idea as absurd. This was what happened when the nations were converted

---

* From the above-mentioned tractate, " Ueber den Beweis des Geistes und der Kraft."

to Christianity. What was it that led men to cast away idols and to worship one God, Maker and Upholder of the world, and to believe in the life eternal, with such firmness that fear of death was utterly banished from their breasts? It was the Christian body of facts, recorded in the Gospels ; the belief in Jesus Christ incarnate, crucified, risen, for the world's salvation. It was not, as has been well pointed out, a fine scheme of truths of reason, such as that God is one, and that the human soul is immortal, which made the early Christians so obstinate in their resistance to temptations to apostasy, and so brave to endure martyrdom. "The stress of that compulsion which carried so many men, women, and youths through the endurance of tortures, even to death, and which brought so many apostates, pallid and trembling, to the tribunals, there to clear themselves, at the cost of their souls, of the fatal suspicion—this compulsion sprang wholly from the perfect conviction they had of the certainty of that *body of facts*, which constituted, and in which consisted, their religious belief. The body of facts, not an opinion of the truth of principles, was the impulsive cause of that endurance of suffering."* So notoriously true is this that it is hard to believe that Lessing was seriously persuaded of the truth of those facts which he sought to isolate from his philosophical and theological creed. Believe the resurrection of Christ, and yet retain one's preconceived ideas of God, say those of Spinoza, to which, according to the testimony of Jacobi, Lessing was more than half inclined? Impossible! Spinoza did

---

* "The Restoration of Belief," p. 66.

not believe in the resurrection of Christ, and he well
knew why; his idea of the essence of God made it
impossible that he should.   Lessing did not with his
whole heart believe in Christ's resurrection any more
than Spinoza; else he could not have imagined it possible to treat such an event as one having no speculative significance, no bearing on the theory of the
universe.   The true attitude of Lessing towards the
"facts" of Christianity comes out towards the end of
the treatise already referred to, where he states that
he believes Christianity for its own sake quite irrespective of the question whether the history related
in the Gospel be true or not.   The moral truths of
Christianity are the ripe fruit of so-called miracles and
prophecies.   Why should I not satiate myself with
them?   What does it matter to me whether the tale
be false or true; the *fruits* are excellent.

So it comes to this at last; let us take the moral
essence of Christianity which commends itself to our
minds, and trouble ourselves no more about the history.   The history is but the shell, this is the kernel;
let us enjoy the sweetness of the kernel, and throw
the shell without regret aside.   But the question is:
Does the kernel remain, after the so-called shell is
cast away?   It may, on the eighteenth-century idea
of what the kernel consisted in; abstract ideas of reason, about God, duty, and immortality; or on the notion of Christianity current in our own day, as consisting simply in an ethical spirit.   But if, as we have
contended all through, it be God manifesting Himself
in grace, then we cannot part with the shell without
at the same time parting with the kernel. *Self-revealing grace is history, or it is nothing at all.*   It is

supernatural facts to begin with working themselves into the course of human history, originating great historical movements not otherwise to be accounted for. In short, it is not a case of kernel and shell. It is a case rather of stone fruit, like a cherry or a peach, from which you cannot remove the stone without fatally injuring the fruit. You may think the history a mere useless stone that may be cast away without loss. But in extracting the stone you wound the tender flesh, and through the wound the precious juice escapes.

9*

THE FUNCTION OF PROPHECY IN REVELATION.

CHAPTER V.

THE FUNCTION OF PROPHECY IN REVELATION.

IN the older apologetic, as I observed at the commencement of last chapter, prophecy takes rank with miracles as an evidential sign attached to a doctrinal revelation. In this connection stress is, of course, laid chiefly on the miraculous element in prophecy. The prophets are conceived of as foretellers of things to come, and their prophecies as miracles of foreknowledge, giving proof that they were entitled to speak to men in God's name as authoritative teachers. In this evidential way of regarding prophecy much of what was most characteristic in the work of the prophets falls into the background. The great business of the apologist is not to find out the prophet's place and function in the history of revelation, and with reference to his own time, but simply to discover as many as possible specific predictions which can be shown to have been accomplished in subsequent history. It is, obviously, a matter of indifference to this argument what the subject of prophecy may be. The particular prediction may be one analogous to the miracle of changing a pen into a pen-wiper, a mere prodigy of foreknowledge, it will still serve the purpose of revealing the presence of a supernatural element. Such a way of regarding prophecy degrades it to a level with heathen divination, and hence it has justly fallen into discredit with recent writers of unexceptionable orthodoxy. By no one has it been more emphatically repudiated than by the late Principal Fairbairn, who in his excellent work on Prophecy speaks of the habit of treating prophecy merely as a branch of the evidences, taking account of nothing but what it contains of the miraculous, as having "impoverished much of our prophetical literature, and stricken it with the curse of barrenness." The statement is strictly true, nor does it tell the whole truth as to the mischief wrought by the narrow and one-sided view so energetically condemned. The exclusively evidential use of prophecy exercises a most serious disturbing influence within the provinces of criticism and interpretation. Its interest being to multiply the number of remarkable specific predictions, its bias in all questions of date and authorship is to adopt, without regard to the state of the evidence, that view which makes the writing contain the largest amount of the miraculous. Then, as the force of the argument depends largely on the explicitness with which the predicted event is preannounced, the apologetic bias naturally inclines to that way of interpreting individual prophecies which makes them like history written before the event—clear, definite, unmistakable—and fosters generally a misconception of the prophetic style which opens the door to a fanatical and irrational mode of interpreting unfulfilled prophecy fitted to bring the whole prophetic literature into contempt—the appropriate territory of theological quacks, to be shunned by all

sensible men.   In the special department of Messianic
prophecy the tendency of the evidential school is to
disregard entirely the historical method of interpretation, and to adopt that view of the prophecies which
makes them obviously and exclusively refer to Christ.
No good can come out of this apologetic special
pleading even to the cause in whose interest it is
practised.   Its only effect is to give such writers as
Mr. Arnold an opportunity to turn the whole argument into ridicule, an opportunity of which the author
of " Literature and Dogma " has fully availed himself.   In his ironical patronising way he says : " It
must be allowed that while human nature is what it
is, the mass of men are likely to listen more to a
teacher of righteousness, if he accompany his teaching by an exhibition of supernatural prescience.   And
what were called the 'signal predictions' concerning
the Christ of popular theology, as they stand in our
Bibles, had and have undoubtedly a look of supernatural prescience.   The employment of capital letters and other aids, such as the constant use of the
future tense, naturally and innocently adopted by interpreters who were profoundly convinced that Christianity needed these express predictions, and that
they *must* be in the Bible, enhanced certainly this
look ; but the look, even without these aids, was sufficiently striking."*   It is a flippant caricature of the
" Argument from Prophecy," but there is just enough
truth in it to make one sensible of the necessity of
forming a conception of prophecy which can be made
subservient to the purposes of apologetic without hav-

---

* Page 110.

ing recourse to the exegetical devices held up to ridicule. This accordingly is the task to which we have now to address ourselves, as the first step in our endeavour to ascertain the function of prophecy in the history of revelation.

The most outstanding feature of prophecy, then, to which all others must be subordinated, and by which all others are best understood, is its *ethical* character. The prophets were not principally foretellers, or prognosticators of future events ; and whatever predictions occur in their writings, and whatever use can be made of these for evidential purposes, the *raison d'être* of this remarkable class of religious teachers was not to supply materials for the apologist. The prophets were before all things preachers of righteousness and mercy to Israel, specially to their contemporaries in Israel. Any one can satisfy himself of this simply by an attentive reading of the prophetic books, with open unprejudiced mind. Everywhere we find these prophets, from Isaiah to Malachi, sternly reproving sin and threatening sinners with condign punishment ; exhorting to obedience to the Divine will, and promising the reward of prosperity to those who do well, and striving to cheer the hearts of those who fear God in evil times, by drawing bright pictures of better days to come. And in all they say and do in fulfilment of their vocation, their obvious aim is to make a moral impression on the men among whom they live. As preachers of righteousness and grace they utter predictions, telling men what will be the reward or the penalty of their conduct under the government of a righteous God, and what good is in store for the world in connection with the purposes of Divine love. But in uttering their predictions they have in view not men living in ages after using these as arguments for the truth of revelation, but people nearer themselves, sinners and saints living in the same land as their neighbours and fellow-countrymen. They are emphatically preachers to their own time, and they express themselves in the language best fitted to impress their contemporaries, depicting the future in colours adapted to their circumstances, so that from their style you can form a guess as to their age. Is the evil of the present disunion? they represent the future as bringing back national unity and peace; is it the misrule of ungodly kings? then the blessing promised is a King who shall reign in righteousness. Is the burden under which Israel groans the heavy yoke of a conqueror? the consolation offered is the advent of a time when the oppressed shall go free, and exercise dominion on their oppressors. Is the curse of the present captivity in a foreign land? the comfort for the afflicted people is the good tidings of approaching restoration proclaimed by one crying in the wilderness, " Prepare ye the way of the Lord, make straight in the desert a highway for our God." Is the heart of Israel heavy because the holy and beautiful house where her fathers worshipped God is burned with fire, and the altar and the daily sacrifice is taken away? the prophet seeks to revive her drooping spirit by a gorgeous description of a new temple, where offerings shall be presented to Jehovah by a holy priesthood in behalf of a grateful penitent people. Evermore the future is described so as to suit the present need, and harmonize with the surroundings and the hopes and fears of the men to whom the prophetic message is primarily addressed, and on whom it is meant to act as a source of inspiration.

This mode of speaking, this way of depicting the future in terms suggested by the present, is manifestly congenial to the *ethical.* character I have ascribed to prophecy. Those who wish to influence their age must speak to the age in language which it can understand, sympathize with, and be moved by. Hence arises a necessity for the prophet, in speaking of the future, to describe it, not as it shall be in all respects, but as those whom he addresses would wish it to be. On this principle our Lord acted when He promised to His disciples that they should sit on thrones judging the twelve tribes of Israel. It was a way of saying: Ye shall have a place of importance in the kingdom of God, suited to their present ideas, and therefore fitted to inspire hope. A more exact, less sensuous, mode of expressing the truth would have made little impression on their minds. Our Lord, knowing that His language conveyed but a rude idea of the actual fact, nevertheless used it, because His aim was not only to predict, but to produce a moral impression. Whether the prophets knew that the future would not correspond closely to their picture is another question. Probably they did not. But whether they did or not, it is certain in any case that their language is figurative and pictorial, and that their prophecies are far enough from answering to the description of prophecy given by Bishop Butler, when he characterized it as " nothing but the history of events before they come to pass."*

* ' Analogy," Part II., chap. vii.

Prophecy justly describable in these terms would certainly serve apologetic purposes excellently well. It would have been very gratifying to the professed apologist to have had at his command prophetic descriptions of the future written in such plain explicit realistic terms, that the correspondence between prediction and fulfilment should be self-evident and undeniable. It is certain, however, that the fact for the most part is not so, and that many of the prophetic oracles are couched in such terms as almost exclude the possibility of literal fulfilment. From the apologetic point of view this is disappointing; but when we consider the subject from the ethical standpoint we feel that the prophetic style is in harmony with the chief end of prophecy. And this suggests the remark that the two views of prophecy, the apologetic and the ethical, are not only distinct, but to a certain extent mutually exclusive. The more prophecy is fitted by its style to serve the ultimate apologetic use, the less it is fitted to serve the immediate parenetic purpose; and conversely, the better it is fitted to make a moral impression on those to whom it is immediately addressed, the less likely is it to supply the apologist with convincing arguments wherewith to silence gainsayers. It is important to understand this law, because failure to do so may lead us into serious error in one or other of two opposite directions. On the one hand, observing the non-correspondence between many of the prophecies and any events lying behind us in the course of history, we may with a certain school of interpreters expect a literal fulfilment in the future, even in cases when the very idea of such fulfilment is grotesque. On the other hand, believing such literal fulfilment to be now impossible, and observing that no such fulfilments took place at the time when they might have been possible, except to a very limited and inadequate extent, we may rush to the conclusion of sceptical critics, that there is nothing supernatural in prophecy, and regard the prophetic oracles simply as glowing idealising pictures of the future drawn by men of ardent poetic temperament, very natural and very beautiful, but without any foundation in reality. At the present time the latter of these two errors is the one chiefly to be guarded against. It is specially important, therefore, to bear in mind that if many of the prophecies have not been and never will be fulfilled in the sense in which they would naturally be understood when they were uttered, the reason is not to be sought in the impossibility of supernatural knowledge, but in the nature of the prophetic vocation. However real the supernatural may be, the prophets could not have spoken to purpose otherwise than they did; therefore the fact of their speaking so cannot legitimately be cited in proof that the supernatural element is a chimæra. The prophetic style is undoubtedly such as to make it possible for writers of naturalistic proclivities, with a certain measure of plausibility, to represent the prophetic delineation of the future as " a kind of fairy tale " which the prophets told themselves and their fellow-countrymen for consolation under distressing circumstances ; very pathetic, and very natural, " having the rights of poetry, but having no pretensions to prosaic truth and reality."* There

* So Mr. Arnold.

is so much plausibility in the representation as to make it very difficult, if not impossible, to convince an unbeliever in the supernatural that he is in error. But by bearing duly in mind the nature of the prophetic calling, we may at least keep ourselves from being imposed on by naturalistic plausibilities, while going a considerable way in agreement with unbelieving interpreters as to the actual characteristics of the prophecies. We can believe it possible that in these oracles a Divine supernatural element is immanent, a genuine vitally important message from God by the mouth of His prophets to us on whom the ends of the world are come, though, it may be, couched in words which, as understood by their contemporaries, and possibly even by themselves, were a very rude adumbration of the reality.

To those who read the prophecies only with an eye to apologetic or edifying uses, such a view will doubtless appear unsatisfactory, and those who entertain it may even seem liable to the suspicion of being in secret sympathy with rationalism. The fear of this, however, must not be permitted to arrest honest endeavour to ascertain by an inductive process the actual characteristics of Hebrew prophecy. We may rest assured that though the result of such an inquiry may be to introduce considerable modifications in the method of proving revelation, it will not be to rob us of revelation itself. The whole subject of prophecy needs reconsideration in order to rescue it at once from the sacrilegious hands of unbelief, and from the irrational treatment which it has often received at the hands of faith ; and to those who undertake this arduous task let us give a hearty God-speed. The work is only just commencing, and the Church may have to wait long before it is accomplished. Already, however, some things have become tolerably clear and gained general acceptance among believing theologians of the new prophetic school. In common with theologians of the naturalistic school, like Kuenen, they hold what is called the *organic* or *historical* theory of prophecy, according to which the prophetic oracles were addressed to the present, were rooted in the present, were expressed in language suited to the present, and pointed to a good in the near future forming a counterpart to present evil, or to an evil in the near future which was to be the penalty of present and past sin. But they hold likewise, and here they part company with the unbelieving interpreter, that a large part of prophecy had a divinely intended reference to the Christian era, that is, was pervaded by a more or less pronounced Messianic element. Yet they do not allow the Messianic aspect of prophecy to overshadow the immediate historical sense, but regard that sense as something to be ascertained irrespective of the sense which we learn to put on prophecy in the light of the New Testament. In the words of a most distinguished member of the school : " It is only when we survey, from the standpoint of the fulfilment of the counsels of God in Christ Jesus, the whole of Old Testament prophecy and the progress of its historical development, that we can come to a full understanding of the teleological significance of any single prediction, but what we gain by this means is a determination of the relation of prophecy to its fulfilment, not an explanation of the contents of the prophecy itself."* It is held that what we do not learn until the period of fulfilment cannot be in the prophecy itself; that the meaning first given to prophecy when considered in the light of fulfilment, and the sense in which the prophets themselves and their contemporaries understood it, that is, the historical sense, must be regarded as perfectly distinct.

Out of the organic conception of prophecy as advocated by Riehm and others, arises naturally the view that the representations of the future given by *successive* prophets are not separate fragments of one picture capable of being combined into a harmonious whole, but rather independent pictures, or to use another figure, successive steps in the growth of an organism. The opposite view is that advocated by theologians belonging to the older school of prophetic interpretation, such as Hengstenberg. Hengstenberg's theory was, that revelations were made to the prophet in a state of ecstasy; that he saw the future in a vision, that in vision he saw events of the remote future as well as of the near, but without any perspective indicating distance; that the historical colouring drawn from the present was *mere* colouring, figurative language understood to be of no importance, so that the sense which results after the colouring has been rubbed off is the true meaning of the prophecy and of the prophet; that while it was possible for any one prophet to see in vision the full picture of the future, each prophet described only a part, so that the total picture is to be got by piecing together all the separate parts. In opposition to this

---

* Riehm, "Messianic Prophecy," pp. 6–8.

ingenious theory, it is contended by the new school that ecstasy was not the only or the usual condition of the prophet when he received revelations; that a vision was not the principal medium of revelation, but rather thoughts already existing in the prophet's mind brought into distinct consciousness by the Spirit of God; that the prophet's view was restricted to the near future, and that he expected the speedy accomplishment of his prophecy while remaining ignorant of the day and hour; that the terms in which he described the future were not regarded by him as mere colouring, to be rubbed off in order to get at the essential element of the prophecy; and that the successive representations of the future given by different prophets were each severally distinct wholes, *the* future, not a mere aspect of it, as seen by the individual prophet. The two theories are very diverse, and without deciding dogmatically between them I may remark that, from the co-existence of such widely divergent views as to the nature of prophecy, each supported by able advocates, it is evident that there is ample scope and urgent need for painstaking, patient investigation. To emphasize this fact, and to protest against premature dogmatism, seems to be the chief duty of the hour, and it cannot be more effectually done than in the words of one whose own contributions to prophetical studies well entitle him to speak with authority. " It is," says Bertheau, " a problem of theological science, by a strict examination of all the phenomena connected with Old Testament prophecy, to lay the foundations for a doctrine as to the nature of prophecy, and to fix the general principles corresponding to the historical state of the case, according to which the rich and manifold expression of the prophetic spirit and the living forms of prophecy can be exhibited and arranged. The problem is not yet solved, nor will it be soon. With the words, ecstasy, vision of an image, with the demand to conceive the prophets as describers of pictures, the formula is not found by use of which the door may be opened to the hidden depths of prophecy."*

Among the questions relating to prophecy on which much diversity of opinion yet obtains is that as to the conditional or unconditional character of the prophetic representations of the future. Did the prophets predict what they believed certainly should be, or only what would be in given circumstances? The question is forced on us by the consideration that many of the prophecies as matter of fact were not fulfilled. What account is to be given of these unfulfilled prophecies? Are we to say simply that the prophets in these instances were mistaken? This is in effect the solution offered by the naturalistic school. The prophets were earnest believers in the moral government of God, and therefore were firmly persuaded that under that government every man and nation would be dealt with according to deserts. Hence they confidently predicted prosperity for all who did right, and ruin for all that did wrong. In so far as there really is a moral order in the world their predictions would come true, but as the moral order is far from perfect,—little more indeed than a *tendency*,—it was a matter of course that prophetic

---

* " Jahrbücher für deutsche Theologie," vol. iv., p. 607.

expectations should often be falsified by events. The prophets in their predictions reasoned from premises only very partially true, and their conclusions, therefore, were as often wrong as right.* Other writers, admitting the facts thus unceremoniously accounted for, explain them by insisting on the conditional character of prophecy. On this view all the promises of future good to Israel would have been fulfilled had Israel complied with the prescribed conditions. All prophecies relating to the chosen people are conditioned by the two principles: "Zion shall be redeemed with judgment, and her converts with righteousness," and "there is no peace to the wicked." The failure of many prophecies promising good to Israel is sufficiently explained by the sad complaint, "Oh that thou hadst hearkened to My commandments, then had thy peace been as a river, and thy righteousness as the waves of the sea." Had Israel hearkened to God's commandments, every good word of God spoken to her by the prophets would surely have come to pass.† This view is certainly very congenial to the *ethical* character of prophecy. It was congruous to the vocation of the prophet as a preacher of righteousness to his time to make the fulfilment of his prophecies dependent on the good behaviour of the people, and there can be no doubt that in many instances he consciously did so. No one who has not a pet theory to defend, like Heng-

---

* So Kuenen, and, to a certain extent, Riehm, though not belonging to the naturalistic school.

† So Bertheau in "Jahrbücher für deutsche Theologie," vol. iv., p. 344.

stenberg, who had but one object in view, viz., to play the part of champion of supranaturalism, will dream of disputing the point. It may, however, very legitimately be doubted whether the theory of conditionality explains all the facts; whether we may say without qualification that had Israel done what God required, all the promised blessings would have been bestowed on her exactly as foretold. It is at least a feasible suggestion, that limitation of prophetic vision must be taken into account in explanation of the non-fulfilment of such prophecies as promised to penitent Israel the reunion of the two kingdoms into one, the complete recall of the Babylonish captivity and the restoration of all the exiles to their own land, the conversion or subjection of all the surrounding nations, so that the chosen people might dwell in safety, with no envious or malicious neighbours to make her afraid.*

Whether prepared to go this length or not, all sober and unprejudiced students of prophecy must at least acknowledge the presence of a conditional element in the prophetic picture of the future. The truth seems to be, that there are two classes of prophecies, one conditional, the other unconditional, or conditioned only as to time and mode of accomplishment. A further fact of importance to be noted is, that in these two classes of prophecy, the prophet appears in two distinct attitudes. In the conditional prophecies he appears as the prophet of *moral law*, in the unconditional as the prophet of *grace*. The vocation of the prophet is not fully understood unless

---

* So Riehm, "Messianic Prophecy," p. 154.

he be regarded under this twofold aspect: as exercising a function on the one hand in relation to God as moral Governor, on the other in relation to God as the God of a gracious purpose. The prophets were at once preachers of righteousness, asserting the reign of moral law over all men; and preachers of a gospel, proclaiming a sovereign purpose of grace that should certainly be fulfilled irrespective of human conduct,—a purpose concerning Israel in the first place, but not exclusively,—a purpose to bless Israel that she might be a blessing to the whole earth. The two functions, as actually exercised, were intimately blended together, but they are in nature distinct, and may be regarded apart. To the prophecies uttered by the prophet as the preacher of Divine grace belong those distinctively denominated *Messianic;* to the prophecies of law and righteousness belong those which pre-announce the destinies of nations and cities, such as Babylon, Egypt, Nineveh, and Tyre. In all the latter class of prophecies is proclaimed, with sublime emphasis, the eternal truth that there is indeed a moral order of the world, that verily there is a God that doeth righteousness in the earth. It is in this aspect of their vocation that the Hebrew prophets are an object of intense interest to such writers as Carlyle and Arnold, who, while making no profession of faith in a supernatural revelation, have a firm belief in a Power in the world making for righteousness. Such cherish and express a sincere respect for those ancient preachers of eternal duty, and fearless denouncers of iniquity, who kept telling their contemporaries of all classes that God's will must be done, and could be disobeyed only under terrible

penalties. They are not even unwilling to admit
that, in their capacity of preachers of righteousness,
the prophets uttered some remarkable predictions
which were substantially fulfilled. Men like the Hebrew prophets, it is acknowledged, can divine, for
there really is a moral order of the world, and men
who with their whole soul believe in it, and who understand the moral phenomena of their age, may to
a certain extent, sometimes even to a surprising extent, read the future in the present. Thus the predictions of doom, subsequently fulfilled, admitted to
be genuine, are resolved into natural products of insight into, and faith in, the laws which regulate the
moral government of mankind. Believing students
of prophecy, while conceding that some predictions
may be thus accounted for, deem it impossible to reduce all to mere displays of sagacity, and see in certain outstanding oracles the undeniable results of
supernatural enlightenment, supplying materials for
a cogent apologetic argument. The argument is competent, but after the most has been made of it, it is
not the one to which the foremost place is due. The
most inviting and fruitful field for the apologist is the
region of Messianic prophecies, embracing under that
head all those in which the *pia desideria*, the hopes,
the ideals of the godly in Israel find expression,
those, in other words, which embody what has been
called the *Hebrew Utopia*. So defined they are a
large group, endlessly varied in character, and of un-
paralleled beauty and interest, the most remarkable
utterances of the kind in the whole literature of mankind. Believers and unbelievers alike acknowledge
the incomparable charm of these Hebrew oracles of

faith and hope, but to very different intents. Unbelief sees in them merely fairy tales which the prophets told themselves to comfort their hearts under the sorrows of the present; *Aberglaube*, extra belief rendered natural if not necessary by the shortcoming of the moral order of the world from the ideal of a perfect moral government. The power that makes for righteousness does not make all the righteous happy, and all the wicked miserable. The prophets seeing this, and unable to reconcile themselves to the actual moral order as the best possible, or to be looked for, invented a system of compensations in the future in the form of a perfect Divine kingdom, a Messiah, and a life to come. Behold the Messianic prophecies! Very beautiful, and having the rights and the worth of poetry, but nothing more, being mere added beliefs born of undying hope, through which—

> " Mercy gave to charm the sense of woe,
> Ideal bliss that truth could never know."

So regards Messianic prophecy, Mr. Arnold, naturally enough from his point of view, according to which the one idea in the Bible is the Power making for righteousness. On that view the truly valuable part of the prophetic literature is that which asserts, with passionate earnestness, the reality of the moral order of the world. All that remains, the so-called Messianic element, must be relegated to the category of poetic invention, valuable chiefly as showing how deep and strong was the faith of the prophets in the power that worketh for righteousness. Undoubtedly, even on this view there is much in the prophetic books of perennial importance to mankind; and, as

I said before in connection with miracles, so I say here in connection with prophecy: it may be a good service to the world to show what a valuable book the Bible will be, even when faith in the supernatural has finally forsaken the earth. But as the Bible is a very different book in its whole scope and aim, according as you exclude or retain the miracles, so is it a very different book according to the view you take of Messianic prophecies. If you regard these simply as fairy tales, then the prophets will speak to you only of righteousness. If, on the other hand, you regard these prophecies as a system of ideals, shadowing forth a *summum bonum* destined to be essentially realized, then the prophets will speak to you of Divine grace as well as of Divine righteousness, and what they say as preachers of grace will no longer be regarded as mere poetic inventions, but as genuine oracles uttered by Divine inspiration. In this light does faith regard the Messianic prophecies, as ideals essentially realized in Christianity, and in these prophecies so regarded it finds not merely an important contribution to the argument for revelation, but a most important constituent part of revelation itself viewed as the self-manifestation of God in grace.

The last observation conducts us to the proper subject of this chapter, viz., the function of Hebrew prophecy in connection with revelation. A full discussion of this topic would require us to consider prophecy under a twofold aspect; not only as related to the promise, but also as related to the law. The latter aspect having already been incidentally referred to, I content myself here with a few observations on a single point connected therewith. One great service rendered by the prophets in connection with the law, was the assertion of the supreme importance of the moral element in comparison with the ritual, in opposition to the prevailing tendency to place the ritual above the ethical. What a prominent place the protest against this tendency held in the prophetic world, is manifest from the most cursory perusal of the prophetic writings, which abound with passages whose burden is, "to obey is better than sacrifice." In such utterances the prophets were the pioneers of Christianity as the religion of the spirit ; and the preparers of a religious revolution whose issue was to be the abolition of ritualism, and the inbringing of the worship of the Father in spirit and in truth. The prophets themselves were not in conscious conflict with the ritual law, but only with the undue importance attached to it in comparison with the great matters of duty as set forth in the Ten Words. They looked on sacrifices and religious ceremonial generally simply as promises to pay the sterling gold of obedience ; and what they could not endure was that promises should be put in place of performance, should be supposed to be performance. But while this is true, there can be little doubt that by their energetic protest against the superstitious overvaluing of ritual, the prophets were unconsciously heralding the advent of a time when the relation between God and His people should be of a purely spiritual character. There are even traces of a clear conscious insight into the truth that ritualism could not be the final form of religion. Perhaps the most distinct is to be found in Jeremiah's oracle of the

new covenant, in which three blessings are specified
as the characteristic marks of that covenant in comparison with the Sinaitic one: viz., God's law of duty
written on the heart instead of on stone tablets as
in the old covenant; the knowledge of God so simplified that one should not need to tell his brother
wherein it consisted; and the full and perpetual forgiveness of sin. The second of the three blessings
points, I think, to the abolition of the ritual law, and
the reduction of religion to the simplest and purest
spiritual service.* In making these remarks I do not
prejudge the critical question as to when ritual took
its final shape in a written form. It is enough for
my purpose if, as may safely be assumed, an oral law
relating to religious service, which men could learn
from the priest's lips, was in existence long before
the prophetic period, and even from the times of
Moses.

Passing from this topic to speak of the function of
prophecy in relation to the promise, I remark that
there is every reason to think that the prophets believed in a gracious purpose of God towards Israel,
and felt it to be an important part of their duty to
keep Israel in mind thereof, by way of consolation
in adversity and strengthening against temptation to
apostasy. One broad fact, which everywhere obtrudes
itself on our attention in reading their writings, is
enough to settle the point. The prophet's eye is
ever turned towards the future; his heart seeks
consolation, not in the memories of the past, but in

* For a statement and defence of this view, see an article by
me in the *Expositor*, vol. ix, on *Jeremiah's Oracle of the New Covenant*.

10

the hope of better days to come. In this respect the Hebrew prophet stands in marked contrast with the prophets and poets of other peoples. The golden age of Pagan poetry lies behind; the golden age of Hebrew prophecy lies ahead, in the future. The contrast deserves consideration in connection with the naturalistic hypothesis, that necessity was the mother of prophetic hopes. Unhappy in the present, the spirit sought refuge in an imaginary better after-age. A plausible theory indeed; but why did not the same law operate in all similar cases? Why does not necessity produce ideal hopes in all peoples suffering under calamities? The exceptional fact seems to demand an exceptional cause; and what more satisfactory explanation can be given than that the prophets knew of a Divine purpose towards Israel, and through her towards the world, which they believed would certainly be fulfilled? or, to put it more definitely, that the call of Abraham and the promise to Abraham were for them objects of firm faith? If we assume this, the whole matter becomes very simple. Then we can understand how, while regarding themselves as ministers of righteousness, they should regard themselves as still more ministers of grace. Especially can we understand how, when on a review of the past history of the nation, they saw everywhere traces of a break-down of the Sinaitic covenant—the nation faithless to God, God visiting a faithless nation with punishment—they should turn with increasing predilection from law to promise, and find in the latter a ground of hope which they now despaired of finding in the former. May we not see the evidence of such a mental attitude in

the words with which Micah closes the book of his
prophecy: "Who is a God like unto Thee, that par-
doneth iniquity, and passeth by the transgression of
the remnant of His heritage? He retaineth not His
anger for ever, because He delighteth in mercy. He
will turn again, He will have compassion upon us;
He will subdue our iniquities; and Thou wilt cast
all their sins into the depths of the sea. Thou wilt
perform the truth to Jacob, and the mercy to Abraham, which Thou hast sworn unto our fathers from
the days of old."[*] Naturalistic criticism tells us that
the "truth to Jacob" and the "mercy to Abraham"
had no objective reality, but were subjective products
of the prophetic spirit, written into the ancient history.[†] Unbelievers in the supernatural need to take
up this position; but on this view prophetism re
mains a phenomenon unexplained. The course of
Israel's religious development is, as has been well
said, *top-heavy;* the overgrowth of prophecy being
too great for the root assigned to it in the early
ages.[‡]

Coming at a time when the gospel of the promise
was needed, and when it was likely to be appreciated,
the prophets whose oracles are recorded in the
prophetic books rendered in various ways important
service, not only as emphatic proclaimers, but more
especially as interpreters, of God's gracious purpose.
They did this, in the first place, by presenting an
idea of God in harmony with that purpose. That

---

[*] Mich. vii. 18–20.

[†] So Pfleiderer, "Die Religion," vol. ii., pp. 337–8. *Vide* extract at p. 81 of this work.

[‡] Smyth, "Old Faith in New Lights," p. 45.

the prophets performed a distinguished part in the development of Israel's idea of God is admitted on all sides. Naturalistic writers even exaggerate the service they rendered in this connection, giving them credit for purging the Hebrew idea of the Divine Being of national particularism, and promoting Jehovah to the honour not merely of supremacy among the Gods, but of sole possession of Deity; in other words, for teaching the world the sublime doctrine of ethical monotheism. This view does less than justice to the ages that went before, inasmuch as there is no good ground for the assertion that, previous to the prophetic era, Jehovah was simply a national God. The contrary is proved by the words of Exodus xix. 5, which Ewald calls the gospel of the Old Testament. "Now therefore, if ye will obey My voice indeed, and keep My covenant, then ye shall be a peculiar treasure unto Me above all people : *for all the earth is Mine;* and ye shall be unto Me a kingdom of priests, and an holy nation." Still it remains true that in the history of revelation one very special function of prophecy was to assert over against idolatrous tendencies, the monarchy of Jehovah, and to set forth with force and vividness the attributes of the one true God, crowning the edifice with the illustrious attribute of grace : so giving to the world an idea of God, which the unknown prophet of the exile justly declares to be Israel's glory.* And having referred to that prophet, I may remark that it is not necessary to travel beyond his prophecies to know what manner

---

* Isaiah lx. 19. "Thy God, thy glory."

of a being Israel's God is. The God of those marvellous oracles is, in the first place, a Creator both
in nature and history, in both spheres bringing into
existence things that previously were not. He is
the Creator of the ends of the earth, and the Maker
of Israel; the Maker also of great characters like
Cyrus, who are raised up at critical periods to play
a signal part in human affairs. He is, further, a
Ruler who has all human destinies under His control,
and who rules over all in righteousness, herein differ-
ing from all the gods worshipped by other Semitic
peoples, who, while also conceived as rulers, Baalim,
were not rulers in righteousness. He is yet again
not only a righteous Ruler, but the *supreme* Ruler, a
Sovereign without a rival. This truth the prophet
proclaims when he represents Jehovah as saying, " I
form the light, and create darkness. I make peace,
and create evil. I, the Lord, do all these things ";
words in which some have discovered a reference to
the religion of the Persians, the good feature of which
was that it believed earnestly in a morally good God,
who loved right and hated wrong, and made all good
things; and its weak feature that it regarded many
things in the world as the workmanship of another
being, who, if not the equal of the good Spirit, was at
least independent of Him, and His perpetual rival;
not deeming it otherwise possible to guard from taint
the moral character of Deity. But the brightest attribute of Israel's God remains to be mentioned. He
is not only a just God, but a Saviour; not only a
Power making for righteousness, but a beneficent
Being who deals not with men after their sins, who,
in sovereign love, forms and executes gracious pur-

poses, and who illustrated this attribute of His character in the election of Israel, and in His whole dealings with Israel in the course of her history down to the date of her captivity in Babylon; and was about to illustrate it anew by a second great act of deliverance. And not only is He a Saviour for Israel, but for the whole world. Israel has been chosen to •be a missionary of the true religion to the whole earth, to be a light to the Gentiles, teaching them how to think of God, and bringing to them the joy of God's salvation. "Look unto Me," saith the God of this prophecy, "and be ye saved all the ends of the earth, for I am God, and there is none else." Jehovah is not the God of the Jews only, but of the Gentiles also; therefore He saith, "Behold Me, behold Me," unto nations that had not hitherto been called by His name.

Here surely was a sublime conception of Deity in which Israel might legitimately boast! It is the glory of the Hebrew prophets to have given adequate expression to Israel's faith. This is honour enough, without claiming for them the credit of originating the idea. This they certainly did not do. The prophets did not create Israel's God, neither did Israel herself create Him. On the contrary, Israel was created, formed into a peculiar people by her God, and taught the knowledge of His character by her marvellous history. God gave to Israel that lofty idea of Himself; gave it not by abstract statements of theological truth, but above all by deeds, by the call of Abraham, by the events connected with the deliverance out of Egypt, and the settlement in Canaan, by the guidance of Israel's history through many crises in subsequent ages. The idea was the reflection of a character manifested in a continuous course of action in the evolution of a gracious purpose. But for this Divine action, not the most gifted of Israel's sons, not even the prophets themselves, had been able to form such a lofty idea of God as we find in the prophetic writings, and especially in those of the later Isaiah, and of Hosea the prophet of Divine love. The idea was not an *invention*, but a revelation made gradually through history, and reaching its full-orbed lustre in the prophetic epoch. I forget not that the prophets were inspired; but their inspiration did not enable them to originate a new idea of God. It rather assisted them to read aright the historical revelation of the Divine name and nature.

A second service rendered by the prophets as ministers of the promise was the proclamation of the truth, so apt to be hidden from Israel's view by her election, that in that promise all nations had an interest. Universalism, the sense of the solidarity of mankind, the conviction that, in spite of all appearances to the contrary, God cared for all peoples, and would ultimately make them all partakers of the blessings of His grace, is, by general acknowledgment, one of the most outstanding and striking characteristics of the prophetic system of thought. In the judgment of naturalistic criticism, this universalism is a prophetic discovery or invention; to one who believes in a revelation of grace, it is simply an emphatic recognition of a truth underlying Israel's vocation from the first. The originality of the prophets here lies not in the discovery of an absolutely new truth, but in the energy with which they grasped, and the

enthusiasm with which they expressed, an old comparatively overlooked one ; and in doing this they
contributed very materially to the better comprehension of God's gracious purpose. For it is beyond
question, as I have already hinted, that the election
of Israel, her vocation to be a peculiar people, in
proportion as it was earnestly believed in, would tend
to foster the conceit that the chosen race had a monopoly of Divine favour ; that, in fact, such a monopoly
was the very meaning of the election. It would be
difficult for members of the peculiar people to understand that election was simply a method, whereby
one was being trained to bless the many. Hence one
of the tasks devolving on the few to whom was revealed the secret of the Lord, would be to teach the
chosen people this lesson, which they were so slow
to understand, and to remind them of the mystery
of love to the Gentiles hid in the Divine bosom.
This task prophets and psalmists faithfully performed,
as is witnessed by beautiful lyrics like the sixty-
seventh and eighty-seventh Psalms, and by many a
golden oracle to be found scattered like gems over
the pages of the prophetic literature. As a fruit of
the same ministry of witnessing to the catholicity of
God's gracious purpose, we may regard some other
portions of the Old Testament, in which one judging
of canonicity by the narrow test of edification might
have difficulty in discovering any claim to form a
part of the sacred collection ; the book of Job for
example. That book has little to teach us; it is remarkable for darkness rather than for light ; we see in
it only certain non-Israelitish men engaged in a comparatively fruitless discussion on the ways of Divine

providence. But if the test of canonicity be, as surely it ought to be, *subserviency to the chief end of revelation*, then the right of the book of Job to a place in the canon cannot reasonably be disputed. For one canonical function, at least, the book certainly does perform, that, viz., of bearing witness to God's interest in men without the pale of the elect nation. A similar observation may be made with reference to the whole *chokmah* literature, the humanistic character of which, evinced by the absence of all distinctively Israelitish reference, may seem at first sight to make its presence in the Hebrew canon an anomaly. The humanism of the chokmah literature is the very ground of its claim to be there, and the very essence of its canonical function, serving, as it does, to remind the chosen people that God was not their God only, to the exclusion of all the rest of the world. On similar grounds we can regard with equanimity critical discussions respecting the literary character of such a book as that of the prophet Jonah. Whether it be history, or whether it be parable, that book bears witness to the catholicity of Divine grace, and in performing that important canonical function, it fully vindicates its title to a place in the literature of revelation.

The greatest service rendered by the prophets, as ministers of the promise, remains to be mentioned. It consisted in conveying an idea of the good to be brought to Israel, and to the world, by the final fulfilment of God's gracious purpose. The oracles in which the nature of the *summum bonum* is foreshadowed, constitute together, as already said, what are called the Messianic prophecies, the name being in strictness applicable to those prophecies only in which the hopes of the future are made to centre in a Person whose sublime mission it should be to satisfy the spiritual longings of humanity, but legitimately and conveniently applied also to all prophecies descriptive of the benefits to be ushered in by the Messianic age. These prophecies are very various in their character, and exhibit the ideal good under almost every conceivable point of view; at least under every point of view naturally suggested by the history and the institutions of the chosen people. The promise to Abraham that his seed should bring blessing to all nations supplied one ready starting-point, and suggested the idea of a world-wide commonwealth, having its centre in Zion, and for its metropolis Jerusalem, and presenting the goodly spectacle of a universal brotherhood, and a catholic Church worshipping One God made known to the ends of the earth by the missionary activity of Israel. Such is the picture of the golden age presented in the psalms above referred to, and in the oracle of *the mountain of the Lord's house,** and in the magnificent description of the latter-day glory, in the sixtieth chapter of Isaiah. Other stems upon which the Messianic hope could be grafted were the institutions of the priesthood and the kingship. Both these institutions might legitimately be brought into connection with the gracious purpose of God towards Israel. For the elect nation, like every other nation, needed organisation, and for its well-being as a state required priests to transact for it in things pertaining to God, and kings to exercise over it just gov-

---

* Isa. ii. 1; Micah iv.

ernment as the visible representatives of the invisible King Jehovah. The prophets recognised the legitimacy of both offices, though they used great freedom in criticising the manner in which priestly and kingly functions were performed by many occupants of office. They could therefore, without impropriety or inconsistency, introduce the ideals of a perfect king and a perfect priest into their picture of the golden age, and the shortcomings of actual kings and priests made such ideals very welcome. Hence we find many of the prophecies take the form of predictions of the advent of a King who should reign in righteousness, and confer upon an oppressed and downtrodden people all the blessings of good government. As a type of this class may be cited the oracle concerning the *rod out of the stem of Jesse.** In that prophecy the Messianic King is connected with the royal house of David. This, as is well known, is a frequently recurring feature in the prophecies in which the ideal takes the form of a king. The reason is, partly that David was the nearest historical approximation to the ideal of a theocratic king, and partly that he had received a promise that his seed should exercise perpetual dominion in Israel.†

There are prophecies of a perfect priest as well as of a perfect king. These may be considered to have their root in the Levitical priesthood, though some of them might conceivably be brought under the category of the Messianic kingship, the priestly office of

* Isa. xi.

† On the reality of this Promise, *vide* "Old Testament Prophecy"; the Warburton Lectures for 1876-1880. By Rev. Stanley Leathes, D.D. Lectures v. and vi.

Messiah being regarded as an attribute belonging to Him as a King. In this view the theocratic king is not only the representative of the invisible ruler, but the representative of the people before God. As Israel was a kingdom of priests, He in whom the nation culminated might not inappropriately be endowed with the highest priestly honours. On this principle the remarkable oracle concerning the Melchisedec priesthood has been interpreted as referring in the first place to one of Israel's historical kings.* One advantage resulting from this view is, that when the priesthood is included under the kinghood, there is less risk of the Messianic prophecies being supposed to refer to different persons; the two ideals may then most naturally be conceived as meeting in one person. But there certainly are some prophecies in which the priestly order appears distinct from the kingly. This holds true especially of the latest prophecies, *e.g.*, those in Zechariah. There, beside Zerubbabel, a descendant of David, stands the high priest Joshua, in a position of honour altogether novel; and, corresponding to that position, Messiah is represented as a Priest in whom the ideal of that sacred office is realized, in the oracle of *the Branch*.† In this prophecy it remains doubtful whether the Messianic priest and the Messianic king are, in the prophet's mind, one person or distinct.

We have thus in the prophetic writings, prophecies foreshadowing an ideal *missionary activity*, an ideal *kingship*, and an ideal *priesthood*, with all that should accompany these good things, a universal religion, a

---

* *E.g.*, by Riehm, *vide* "Messianic Prophecy," pp. 71-3.
† Zech. vi.

kingdom of God, a blessed fellowship between God and man. Whether the first of these ideals, the prophetic, refers to an individual or to a community, and whether the second and third, the kingly and priestly, refer to two persons or to one only, are questions that may legitimately be asked; but all three ideals enter into the prophetic representation of the future. They are not all to be met with in each of the prophets. One gives one, another another, and the close relation between prophecy and history appears in the correspondence between the kind of ideal presented by a particular prophet, and the circumstances of the Hebrew nation when he prophesied. The prophets of the Assyrian period think of the Messiah as a king, finding in Him one who should be able to cope with the great monarchs of the earth. In the prophecies forming the second part of the book of Isaiah, which, whether written at the time of the exile, were at all events written for that time, there is no word of a Messianic king. The "servant of God" of these prophecies is a prophet, whose vocation is to give light to the Gentiles, and who in the discharge of his office is destined to suffer much at the hands of an unbelieving world. After the exile, when the work of engrossing interest was the rebuilding of the temple and the restoration of the temple-worship, the priestly office came to the forefront, and the Messianic ideal took the form of a priest sitting on a throne, and exercising influence with God in behalf of the people.

But while the Hebrew prophets, according to their varying temperaments and circumstances and the diverse revelations made to them, present the Messianic hope under different aspects, they all concur in making on our mind one general impression. With one voice they say: the present form of religion and of the kingdom of God is not the perfect or the final one. The perfect is yet to come; all that has been or is, even in Israel—priesthood, kinghood, religious ritual—is imperfect and therefore transient. The perfect, the religion of the spirit, the true priesthood and kinghood are in the future. In one other thing all agree. They not only say, *the Perfect is yet to come*, but they say, *the Perfect shall come;* the ideal shall be realized. These prophecies of ours are not mere dreams, mere idle tales which we tell ourselves and our brethren to amuse our sad minds. They are the word of the Lord which endureth for ever, and as such they must be fulfilled. If the Scriptures contain the record of a veritable revelation, this prophetic faith ought to be true. For just at this point a marked difference ought to be observable between ethnic and revealed religion. The ideals of Pagan religions may, to a large extent, be poetic dreams, never destined to be realized; but the ideals of revealed religion ought to be realized, and by their fulfilment be proved to be no dreams of the prophet's heart, but revelations from heaven. That these ideals should be enclosed in temporary husks, destined to be cast aside when the era of fulfilment comes, is not a matter to cause surprise.. We will not expect every word of the prophet to be fulfilled to the letter; neither will we lay too much stress on remarkable individual details, looking for exact correspondence between these and events occurring in the era of fulfilment. We will simply ask: have the prophetic expectations been realized in the main, or have they not? Have the new covenant, and the spiritual worship, and the universal religion, and the Divine Prophet, Priest, and King come, or do we still look for them, and look for them in vain?

The short and simple creed of the apostolic Church, that Jesus of Nazareth is the Christ, is an affirmative answer to the question, to the effect that Jesus is the Messiah of Old Testament prophecy, and that in Him and in the religion which He founded all the ancient hopes of the Hebrew nation were essentially fulfilled. This answer the catholic Church in every age has endorsed, and the cordial acceptance thereof is one of the marks by which the position of faith is sharply distinguished from that of unbelief. In confessing this truth all believing theologians are at one ; and the fact is to be emphasised in view of the differences of opinion which prevail among them as to the best method of proving the doctrine accepted in common. On this latter point two widely contrasted views are held. One lays the stress of the argument on the remarkable special predictions concerning the Messiah, such as those relating to the birth from a virgin and the rising up of the Messianic Deliverer out of Bethlehem. On the other view, the wisest method of proof is to begin with the great general outlines of Messianic prophecy, with the aim of showing that in Christ Old Testament ideals are gathered up in a centre and in the highest sense realized, reserving specialties for the conclusion, and using them thus, not as the foundation, but as the copestone of the edifice of faith. This view naturally commends itself to those who are convinced that every one of the special predictions had a primary reference to some historical event or character much nearer the prophet's time; an opinion which, as held by believing theologians, is not meant to deny that these predictions had also a divinely intended reference to Jesus Christ, which, from a doctrinal point of view, may be the more important. But this latter position, as held by the school of interpreters I now speak of, is the effect, not the ground of faith. Having satisfied themselves on other grounds that in Jesus Messianic prophecy is fulfilled, they are prepared to recognise a divinely ordered teleology immanent in all prophetic utterances, a teleology whereof the prophets themselves were, to a great extent, unconscious. Apart from the question of interpretation, this change of front seems best fitted to serve the present interests of apologetic. For unbelief finds it much easier to dispose of the individual predictions on which the older apologists rested their case, than to explain away the correspondence between Christianity and Hebrew prophecy in the great general outlines. The distinction between primary and secondary prophecies—that is, between those whose first and perhaps exclusive reference is Messianic, and those in which a primary reference other than Messianic cannot be denied, and only a secondary reference to Messiah can be maintained—this distinction is very unstable and unsatisfactory. The distinction of course implies that only the primary prophecies can be the basis of faith; and the argument, as between the apologist and his opponent, resolves itself into a wrangle about individual prophecies and their proper interpretation. How un-

satisfactory the issue of this debate is likely to be we
may learn from these words of Mr. Arnold: "Who
will dispute that it more and more becomes known
that these prophecies cannot stand as we have
here given them? . . . . That the passage from Genesis with its mysterious Shiloh, and the gathering of
the people to Him, is rightly to be rendered as
follows: 'The pre-eminence shall not depart from
Judah, so long as the people resort to Shiloh (the
national sanctuary before Jerusalem was won), and
the nations (the heathen Canaanites) shall obey
him.'"* This one instance may suffice as a sample
of the way in which the Messianic reference is eliminated. I do not mean to say that the interpretation
given is right, and that the apologist must yield the
point. There is more probably in many individual
prophecies than the children of the Zeitgeist find.
But if not right, Mr. Arnold's interpretation is at
least plausible; and of all similar cases plausibility
may be predicated to such an extent as leaves the
unbelieving interpreter with a very complacent conviction that he has truth on his side. It is surely
therefore wise to give prominence to the view that
even if all the remarkable special predictions and so-
called primary prophecies were explained away one
by one, there would still remain ample solid ground
on which to construct a weightier, if less simple argument, tending to show that in Christianity we have
the glorious fulfilment of a Divine purpose of grace,
whereof predictive intimations and foreshadowings

---

* "Literature and Dogma," pp. 111–114.

are to be found in every page of Hebrew prophecy, in every glowing picture of the good time coming.

That in Jesus were fulfilled the best aspirations and hope of the Hebrew race is, to a certain extent, admitted by naturalistic critics; but in a way which utterly fails to do justice to the facts. Here, also, Mr. Arnold may be taken as a representative man. In his opinion the fusing together of the various ideals of Old Testament prophecy was a procedure warranted neither by strict interpretation of the texts, nor by any real Divine purpose, but was simply an original stroke of genius on the part of Jesus, a happy audacity. This, however, it certainly was. The bright idea struck Him to take the suffering servant of later Isaiah and make him one with the Messianic King who was to come forth out of Jesse's roots, and with the Son of man coming with the clouds of heaven, and so to set Himself to found a kingdom, not by might nor by power, but by the force of truth and of meekness and patient love. And the idea succeeded, and success justified the audacity and the innovation. Attempts at such a combination of apparently incompatible ideals had been made before, which is not surprising, " for the true line of Israel's progress lay through it. But not he who tries makes an epoch, but he who effects, and the identification which was needed Jesus effected."*

This is plausible, but not satisfactory. It cannot content any thoughtful, serious man, no matter what philosophical school he belongs to, to be told that Christ's success was a happy hit, and His relation to

* " Literature and Dogma," p. 96.

the Old Testament a self-constituted and arbitrary one. One cannot help thinking that the happy combination of Old Testament ideals in Christ's consciousness was grounded on the eternal truth of things, and that His success was the fulfilment of a purpose of the living God, shadowed forth in those prophetic ideals. As to the former point, it is by no means clear that the prophets themselves had no suspicion of the truth that the ideals might meet in one person.* But grant they had not, and that for want of such insight they thought of their ideals as mutually exclusive; may we not regard the combination of these in the consciousness of Christ as the result of a more than prophetic knowledge, and the marvellous success of His work, in spite of its entire contrariety to the spirit of the world, as the experimental proof that the combination was not only legitimate, but divinely intended? Have we not, in fact, in Christ not only the fulfilment of the prophecies, but the filling up of them, the supplement of their deficiency, the last and highest prophecy as well as the realization of all prophecies that went before, gathering their scattered rays into a focus, and yielding a Messiah not one-sided, but all-sided, and proving Him to be the true Messiah just by the union in Him of all prophetic ideals?

Such is the view of the fulfilment of Messianic prophecy which commends itself to those in our day who, while firmly believing with the Church of all ages that Jesus is the God-given Christ in whom His promises are Yea and Amen, nevertheless feel that

---

* *Vide* Isa. liii.; specially ver. 12.

modification of the old argument is demanded by modern criticism and exegesis. They see in Christ and Christianity the flower and fruit, and in ancient prophecy the bud. They see in Jesus of Nazareth and His religion all Old Testament religious ideals realized. Not only so, they see in Christianity more than they believe it possible to see in Hebrew prophecy, apart from the light shed on it by fulfilment. They not only find in prophecy an evidence of Christ's Divine mission, but they find in Christ a key to the understanding of prophecy, a key to the riddle of the ancient oracles, a clear unfolding of what they dimly hinted at. Christianity contains for them all that the prophets taught, and more, "just as the living plant contains the life, and more than the life, of the seed ; just as the day contains the light of dawn and more light. Prophecy is the seed, the twilight glow ; Christianity is the life, the full day."*

According to this view Christ is, in the first instance, His own witness ; and instead of being proved conclusively by prophecy, interpreted apart from the light of the Christian era, to be the Christ, He first enables those who believe in Him to understand aright the prophecies, and to see in the correspondence of these, rightly understood, and His personal character and history, the evidence of a Divine purpose running through the previous ages and finding its fulfilment in Him. And such, indeed, to a great extent, is the actual state of the case. The pro-

---

* Adeney, "The Hebrew Utopia," a Study of Messianic Prophecy, p. 354. An excellent book, by one belonging to the modern school of apologists whose position I have attempted to indicate.

phecies are not such, that by the mere citation of them you can shut a man up to the belief that Jesus of Nazareth is the Christ. They are rather such that when, on other grounds, a man is disposed to receive Jesus as the Lord and Saviour, what in them was enigmatical before, becomes luminous with meaning. The proof from prophecy is not mathematically stringent; a mind not spiritually prepared to feel its force can evade it. For special predictions other fulfilments than those supplied in the life of our Lord can be sought out; and with reference to general prophecies embodying the Messianic ideals, the position can be plausibly taken up, that the ideals were not conceived by the prophets as meeting in one person, could not indeed, being in their nature incompatible. How far prophecy is from being irresistible evidence, is sufficiently apparent from the reception actually given to Jesus by His contemporaries; who, though familiar with the letter of the Hebrew Scriptures, scouted His claim to be the Messiah as altogether preposterous. Even in the case of the few who believed in Him, faith was not the effect of the proof from prophecy. Believers did not first study the prophecies and then come to Jesus as disciples; they first came to Jesus, and then learnt how to interpret the prophecies. The proper interpretation of prophecy was not the cause, but the effect of their faith. And the same thing holds good in the experience of Christians generally. " Prophecy serveth not for them that believe not, but for them which believe."* We come to Christ, drawn

* " It must, however, not be forgotten that the office of prophecy is not to convert, but to convince ; not to lay the foundation, but to confirm those in whom it has already been laid ; for we are told

by His own native attractions, and we learn in His school how to read the Old Testament. It does not follow from this that the prophetic argument is of no value. Prophecy does indeed speak first to faith, but then its deeper meaning is revealed from faith to the production of higher, stronger faith. Prophecy may fail to lead an unbelieving man to Christ; but when one has become a believer, he is confirmed in his faith by the inner harmony between the spirit of prophecy and the doctrine of Christ. And, as his faith grows in intelligence, his sense of the extent to which the testimony of Jesus is the spirit of prophecy becomes deepened. At first he may be impressed only by the correspondence between a few of the broad features of prophecy and the history of Christ and Christianity: the new covenant of Jeremiah's oracle, the spiritual religion insisted on by all the prophets, the extension of the true religion to all nations, the mission of " the servant of Jehovah " as the herald of the new era, and his sufferings in the performance of the duties

---

on sufficiently high authority, that *prophecy serveth not for them that believe not, but for them which believe.* Let us not seek, therefore, to make prophecy, or the study of prophecy, do a work for which perhaps it was not designed. Let us not endeavour to make it sustain or support the whole superstructure of the Christian fabric. That it is one of the converging evidences of the Christian faith we are only too thankful to remember. Let it not be supposed that it is the only one, and let us not reason as if it were. Christianity is an historic religion, and its central weight rests upon a small group of facts, those, for instance, which are gathered together in the Apostles' Creed. If the main facts of the Christian creed are not accepted, it is utterly useless to appeal to prophecy. If we do not accept the verdict of history, we shall certainly reject the testimony of that which claims to have anticipated history."—STANLEY LEATHES' *Warburton Lectures,* pp. 10, 11.

of his high calling. The spirit of prophecy may thus mean, to begin with, the best things, the choice passages in the prophetic writings, containing anticipations of the Christian religion. But by-and-by it comes to mean much more than this—even the soul animating the prophetic oracles from beginning to end ; not merely the flower, but the sap which pervades the whole plant ; not merely a few outstanding passages, but the drift and tendency of the entire literature. The whole Old Testament now appears an organism of which Christ is the final cause. When this position is reached, one can afford to regard with great equanimity discussions as to the meaning of particular predictions, because he understands that " in the argument from prophecy we have to do with a forest, not with a single bough or a basket of leaves ; with the whole trend of a coast, not with the single headlands or inlets of the sea ; with a zone of constellations, not with scattered stars."* And yet, just on that account, he can now believe that even these special predictions for which unbelieving criticism thinks it has discovered a non-Messianic interpretation, have a divinely intended reference to Christ. The remarkable correspondences between some of these predictions and events in the life of Christ, which at first may have seemed purely accidental and surprising, appear now as natural as the correspondence which subsists between the structure of an organism and its environment, or between the features of a son and those of his father. In like manner that the history of Israel, the experiences of individual

* Smyth, " Old Faith in New Lights," p. 248.

members of the chosen race, and the Levitical institutions, should be foreshadowings of the good things
to come with Christ, appears from the viewpoint of
faith not at all incredible. When we have once accepted the doctrine that in Christ was fulfilled a grand
redemptive purpose of God for which all previous
history was a preparation, we cannot have any difficulty in believing that a Divine teleology was immanent in all the outstanding features of Israel's eventual
story: in her religious services, in the lives of her best
kings, in prophetic utterances referring primarily to
events and circumstances connected with the prophet's
own time. Typical meanings of ritual institutions
and double senses of prophecies are doubtless mysterious things, which, in the hands of unwise interpreters, may easily degenerate into the magical and absurd ; but the radical objection of unbelief after all is
not to these, but to that which they presuppose, a
Divine purpose of grace cherished from the earliest
ages, never lost sight of, gradually evolved in the
course of time, and finally reaching its consummation
in Jesus Christ. To none but those who doubt the
purpose is the Messianic reference of the whole Old
Testament a serious stumbling-block.

THE DOCTRINAL SIGNIFICANCE OF REVELATION.

11*

CHAPTER VI.

THE DOCTRINAL SIGNIFICANCE OF REVE-LATION.

IN the first chapter we saw that two diametrically opposed opinions concerning revelation have been entertained: the one, that it is wholly doctrinal; the other, that it has nothing to do with doctrine. The truth lies between these extremes. Revelation, though not in the first instance doctrinal, neverthe-less has a doctrinal significance which was unfolded with increasing clearness as the process of revelation advanced towards its consummation. And not only does it issue in doctrine; it presupposes doctrine. The tree of revelation has a speculative root, as well as a foliage and fruitage of positive truth. Every religion has its own way of looking at God, man, and the world; in other words, reflectively or instinctively every religion has its characteristic theory of the uni-verse. Christianity is no exception. As the religion of redemption it is anything rather than speculative; a fact, not a theory; nevertheless, it presupposes cer-tain views concerning the great subjects of specula-tion, which no one can help cherishing who believes in a revelation of grace, and which can be deduced, *à priori*, from the Divine fact given to faith. If Christianity be true, if it be indeed the case that God has revealed Himself in history as the God of grace, bringing His love to bear as a redemptive force on the sins of mankind, then certain inferences follow concerning God, and concerning the object of His loving care. These speculative presuppositions of the religion of redemption, though not formally taught, are tacitly assumed and everywhere implied in the Scriptures, and may be gathered therefrom by inductive inquiry. But even without consulting the Scriptures we can determine for ourselves the speculative implicates of revelation, so far at least as to be able to answer the question, How does the Christian theory of the universe differ from that of Pantheism, or of Paganism, or of Deism, or of Materialism? My chief aim in this closing chapter, is to vindicate the apostolic assertion that the Bible is profitable for doctrine, that it possesses value not merely as a means of moral and religious edification, but moreover as an aid towards determining the didactic significance of the central fact of revelation. But it may be a useful introduction to the discussion of this thesis, to consider briefly what we can learn for ourselves from the bare idea of revelation as the self-manifestation of God in grace, or of Christianity as the religion of redemption.[*]

Among the self-evident or demonstrable presuppositions of Christianity are the following :—

1. That God is an ethical Personality. The God who reveals Himself as a God of grace cherishes and executes a purpose of love. But to cherish a purpose and to love are acts of a Personal Being.

---

[*] On this subject the reader may consult Delitzsch, " System der christliche Apologetik."

2. That man also is a moral Personality, and occupies a most important place in the universe. He is the object of God's care ; God is mindful of him ; God seeks his love : has for His aim in redemption to establish a fellowship between man and Himself. Man, therefore, must be a person and not a thing, for there can be no fellowship between things, or between a person and a thing, but only between persons.* And as a moral personality man is not merely a part of the world, but stands above the world, supernatural in his being, and possessing the high dignity of a son of God, a dignity which he retains even amid his moral degradation, because even then he is an object of Divine care.

3. That sin is a reality for God ; in other words, that God is a Holy Being. All slight, minimizing, apologetic, optimistic conceptions of sin as a triviality, an infirmity, a necessity, or as the negative side of good—" good in the making "—are incompatible with honest faith in an economy of redemption. Both the theology and the anthropology of this faith exclude such thoughts. Moral distinctions cannot, like binary stars to the unassisted eye of man, be invisible to the eye of a God who has manifested Himself in history as a moral physician. God does not attempt the impossible or the unnecessary ; therefore sin can be neither a fatality nor a trifle to Him. Then the place which faith assigns to man in the universe equally forbids such slighting thoughts of his moral shortcomings. To take a genial view of sin may appear humane, but it is not respectful to the sinner. It is to

---

* Delitzsch pithily remarks that there can be no fellowship between God and the mountains.

treat human nature with contempt, to regard man as a being so weak that it is vain to expect virtue from him ; as a victim of necessity who only deludes himself when he imagines he is free ; as a thing, not a person ; an animal, not a rational being.

4. That God is the Maker of the world, the Creator of matter not less than the Father of our spirits. In the Pagan theory of the universe, matter is eternal, and in a sense independent of God. This view the believer in a religion of redemption cannot accept, for more than one reason. First, because it compromises God's character as personal, and His position as the supreme. Personality demands that God should be independent of the world, and supremacy demands that the world should be dependent on Him. The two demands are satisfied only by the doctrine of creation as involving a beginning of the world. If we suppose the raw material of the world, the ὕλη, to have been eternal, God may still be independent of the world, but He cannot be supreme, for the world exists independently of Him. He is not in that case the Creator of the world, but only the shaper of chaos into a world of order, a *cosmos*. If, on the other hand, we assume an eternal process of creation, so excluding the idea of a pre-existing uncreated ὕλη, then we save the Divine supremacy at the cost of Divine independence. Creation then becomes a process of necessary emanation, excluding freedom, and God becomes confounded with the universe as the original ground out of which all being by an incessant and necessary process flows, the *natura naturans* of Spinoza's system. The alternatives before us are Manichæan dualism or Pantheism. God

is either one of two, or He is not even one; He has not even the privilege which we enjoy of being an independent personality, a whole over against the world; but is either a part of the world, or the world itself under a certain aspect. But a still stronger reason for the doctrine of creation is to be found in the necessity for excluding the notion that matter is the source of moral evil, as incompatible with faith in redemption. If matter be the cause of sin, as Greek philosophy taught, then redemption, as Celsus justly held, is impossible. The only possible redeemer in that case is *Death.* This Pagan doctrine, therefore, must be eliminated if redemption is not to be made void; and the most effectual way to neutralize it is to believe that matter is God's creation, and therefore good, that the Redeemer of man's soul is also the maker of his body, and that, therefore, the latter, so far from being the source of inevitable sin, is itself capable of redemption. This, therefore, the believer in a revelation of grace firmly holds as an essential part of his creed.

The foregoing are amongst the more obvious elements of the Christian theory of the universe. Less certain, yet equally congenial to the central truth of faith, are those which follow.

5. There is a close connection between the moral evil in the world, and the *physical.* What the precise connection is it is rather difficult to determine. It may be hazardous to affirm that physical evil universally is the God-appointed penalty of moral evil. Schleiermacher lays down the position that the collective evil in the world is to be regarded as penalty of sin, social evil directly, natural evil indirectly. The

meaning of the thesis so far as it relates to natural
evil is, that objectively considered such evil is not
caused by sin, but subjectively considered it is the
penalty of sin, because without sin it would not be
felt to be an evil. According to Schleiermacher the
physical world cannot be altered by sin, therefore
death, which belongs to the order of nature, did not
come into the world after sin, but the whole world
appears different in consequence of sin. This view
is certainly in accordance with the genius of Christianity, as a religion which contemplates all things
from an ethical point of view. That religion takes
an ethical view of God, of man, and of human conduct; how congruous to its general way of looking at
things that it should bring the whole aspect of nature under the same category, and regard the present
state of the physical universe as in a pre-established
harmony with the moral condition of its human inhabitants. The hypothesis does not necessarily imply that the order of nature was altered after sin
entered the world; it need imply only that in the
teleology of the creation regard was had in the fram-
ing of nature to the foreseen event of sin. Death,
decay, violence may have been in the world not only
before man sinned, but before man existed. But they
were because he *was to be;* prior in time they were
posterior to man's sin in creative intention. God
made the world, that is to say, such that it might be
a fit abode for a race of morally fallible beings, with
all the materials necessary for their moral discipline,
with evils of diverse sorts to be regarded as penalties
of sin, and also with manifold benefits indicative of
Divine patience, summoning to repentance, and in-

spiring in the penitent hope of pardon. This view of the universe harmonizes best with the tendency of Christianity in all things to subordinate the natural to the moral, as opposed to the religions of heathenism, which subordinate the moral to the natural. It has the further recommendation, that it steers a middle course between Optimism which sees no evil in nature, and Pessimism which sees in it no good; between the rose-coloured theories of the Deists and illuminists of last century, who resolutely refused to see a dark side in nature, and the sombre views of a Schopenhauer, who sees in nature so much evil that the universe might well be mistaken for the work of a devil rather than of a good God. Christianity sees in the world both evil and good: evil because man hath sinned, and God desired that man sinning should discover sin to be a bitter thing; good because God is gracious and dealeth not with men after their sin; the evil and the good bearing witness to two economies of judgment and mercy which, however, are radically only parts of one redemptive economy, working in different ways towards the fulfilment of God's gracious purpose in Christ, to which the whole constitution of nature and the whole course of history are subservient.

6. The present state of things is not final. The faith of redemption teaches us to expect a palingenesis, a renovation of all things, the introduction of a new heaven and a new earth wherein dwelleth righteousness, the advent of an æon when the creation shall be emancipated from the bondage of vanity and corruption, and when her groaning and travailing shall issue in the birth of a renovated world, bring-

ing redemption even to man's body, and completed sanctity to his spirit; bringing renewal not merely to the individual, but to society — not merely to man, but to physical nature. Already Christianity has achieved much; it has caused God's kingdom to come on this earth in at least a rudimentary way, conferring many benefits on humanity, participated in even by those who do not believe in Christ or so much as know His name. It conferred blessing on the world even before Christ's advent, as the hidden ground of God's patient bearing towards our race from the first. But when all has been reckoned up which Christianity has done for men in spiritual and temporal respects, for individuals and society, for Christendom and for Heathendom, for pre-christian and for post-christian ages, it comes far short of what shall be. We look for results more worthy of the love of God, more commensurate with the moral grandeur of the act by which the foundations of the new order of things were laid, more clearly demonstrating that Christ is the centre of the universe, in whom all things both in heaven and in earth are gathered up. We do not, indeed, expect the grand consummation to come soon. For we observe that Providence works leisurely and is never in a hurry, one day being with the Lord as a thousand years to us, so that He takes His promise as calmly the day it is made, as we take events which happened a thousand years ago; and, therefore, our faith does not fail on discovering reason to think that millenniums may elapse before the work of redemption shall have reached its full development. Nevertheless we, according to His promise, look for a new heaven and a new earth wherein dwelleth righteousness. For we observe that this also is a feature of God's providential working : that while He never hurries, He also never forgets ; though He work slowly, yet worketh He surely, a thousand years being to Him as one day to us, so that at the end of a thousand years He remembers and is in earnest with His purpose, as we remember and lay to heart our purposes the very day they are formed.

To these speculative presuppositions of Christianity some add the doctrine of a Fall, and the doctrine of the Trinity. They are certainly both congruous to the central conception of revelation, but it may be doubted whether, apart from the Scriptures, we could deduce them from the mere idea of Christianity as the religion of redemption. Schleiermacher, while regarding Christianity as a state of completed fellow-ship between God and man brought about by Christ, denies that a fall, and by implication an unfallen state, are involved therein. He views Christianity not as a restoration, but as the completion of the first creation, which in his opinion did not culminate in a sinless man, but simply in a human being endowed with the bare rudiments of personality, to whom sin was a certain if not an inevitable experience—a mere matter of course. In advocating this view, Schleiermacher is manifestly influenced by the desire to maintain harmony between faith and the claims of science and philosophy. Nevertheless, it must be admitted to be a perfectly legitimate opinion *from a speculative point of view.* The fact of a Divine interposition for the redemption of mankind from the power of moral evil does not necessarily shut us up to any particular view as to the origin of sin. Schleiermacher's hypothesis for the solution of that hard problem may be false in point of fact, but it is not incompatible with faith in a revelation of grace. As regards the doctrine of the Trinity, when we look at redemption as a completed fact involving the Incarnation, and the institution of the Church as a society animated by Christ's spirit, it is impossible not to feel that, in connection with the revelation of grace, God manifests Himself under a plurality of aspects, as Father, Son, and Spirit. But whether the Trinity so given be a trinity of manifestations or of Persons, a trinity as conceived by Sabellius or the Trinity set forth in the creeds, neither reason nor the Christian consciousness by itself could determine. It is, therefore, only what was to be expected when we find Schleiermacher, whose method of determining what is to be regarded as matter of faith is an appeal to the Christian consciousness, teaching a merely Sabellian Trinity.

Conscious of inability to advance further in our unaided endeavour to ascertain the didactic import of revelation, we gladly turn to that sacred literature which was given by inspiration for instruction and for discipline in righteousness. But here our way is barred by certain moderns, who tell us that it is vain to go to the Bible in quest of objective truth ; one party affirming that the sacred book contains no materials for the construction of any doctrine whatsoever, and was never intended to supply such ; another, while admitting the availableness of the book for doctrinal purposes, denying the absolute truth of any doctrines thence deduced. Of the former class Mr.

Arnold is the best known representative; of the latter, Dr. Mansel. Mr. Arnold carries his agnostic attitude to the extreme length of denying that the Bible teaches us anything concerning God, even that He is personal. God, we are given to understand, is simply a personification of that righteousness to which the temperament of the Hebrew led him to attach a preponderating importance. The fact-basis of the personification was the observation that there is a Power, not ourselves, in the world making for righteousness. This much is implied in the Bible forms of speech, but nothing more; no definite opinion concerning the nature of God, such as that He is personal, or that He is the intelligent Author and Governor of the world. The Bible writers meant to affirm no more than is admitted by Strauss, viz., that there is a moral order of the world; they had no theory as to the cause of this order.

In taking up this position, Mr. Arnold assumes that the only source of information concerning Jehovah, or the Eternal, accessible to the Bible-writers, was nature and ordinary providence. He altogether ignores the miraculous element, and along with that the gracious aspect of God's character whereof the miracles are the fact-basis. But the question is: can we retain these and still affirm that the Bible implies no particular view of the Divine nature and character? That we can legitimately make such an affirmation concerning the Bible, as conceived by Mr. Arnold, is admitted; for on that view the fact-basis of all Scripture representations which are to be regarded as of permanent value is simply that moral order of the world which, as we have seen, is recognised by men of all schools, even by atheists. But can we say the same thing of revelation as we conceive it? We cannot ; for the fact-basis here is not merely the moral order of the world, which forms part of the course of nature, but supernatural manifestations of God, not regarded as facts at all by Mr. Arnold, and which cannot be recognised as facts by any man who is not a theist. Assuming the reality of the fact-basis of the Bible name for God,—the Redeemer,—we learn these things from it. *First*, God is a Being who cherishes purposes, sets Himself ends to be worked out by a process of historical evolution. *Second*, God is a Being who, while usually working according to the course of nature, and always so shaping His action that it shall enter easily and harmoniously into that course, is yet not chained down to the fixed order of things, but is so far above the world, and free in His relation to it, that He can at will produce results which nature itself could not accomplish. In these two inferences combined we have the idea of Personality, so abhorred by Pantheism and so ridiculous in Mr. Arnold's eyes. God has conscious purposes which He freely fulfils, sometimes by natural causes, sometimes by supernatural ; in other words, if we believe the narratives in the sacred book to be historical, we must conceive of God as self-conscious and self-determining, that is, as personal. If we reject the *attribute*, we must reject the alleged facts by which its ascription to God is justified and demanded. That is to say, we cannot with Mr. Arnold deny the Personality of God without also with him mutilating the Bible, and cutting out of it everything miraculous. Of course by the method of mutilation you can make the Bible teach just as little as you like. But if the question be what notion of God is suggested by the Bible, then it must be taken as it stands, and being so taken, it will be found to yield a very different idea of God from that extracted from it by the author of "Literature and Dogma," an idea into which Personality as defined enters as an essential ingredient.

But the Scriptures do not merely teach by necessary and omnipresent implication, that God is personal. They exhibit Him as an ethically perfect Personality. The purposes which the Bible ascribes to God are gracious ones; the acts it represents Him as performing are acts of mercy and faithfulness in the furtherance of a benignant design. The writers have intense faith in the reality of Divine love, and they record facts which supply all the proof of its reality that is possible. It is certainly true that they labour in expression when speaking of Divine love. Mr. Arnold remarks of the language of the Bible, that it is literary, not scientific; words thrown out at an object of consciousness not fully grasped, which inspired emotion. It is a just observation, but not in the sense the author intends. The Bible writers do throw out words at God, very specially when they speak of His love. Paul speaks of heights, depths, lengths, breadths, in connection with Divine love, without indicating to what he refers; crowding thought and intense emotion here, as often elsewhere, making shipwreck of grammar.* Psalmists speak of multitudes of tender mercies, and represent God's mercy as in the heavens. Prophets declare that God multiplies pardons, and

* *Vide* Lightfoot on Galatians, at the place chapter ii. 3-10.

back the daring affirmation by the reflection that in the magnanimity of forgiving love, God rises in His thoughts and ways as far above men as heaven is above the earth. These are samples of phrases thrown out at Divine charity, but not in the sense that they are fine words to which no corresponding reality exists in the Divine nature, but rather in the sense that the Divine reality is great, sublime, beyond conception or expression. A very substantial difference. Mr. Arnold's words thrown out are rapturous phrases flung at a cloud which a man in a heated state of imagination mistakes for a mountain. The phrases quoted from the Bible are uttered by men who find themselves in presence of a veritable mountain range, and who cannot get words that shall adequately express the feelings of admiration awakened by the majestic sight.

Passing from Mr. Arnold to Dr. Mansel, we find him, in his Bampton Lecture on " The Limits of Religious Thought," laying down the position that God cannot be known in the truth of His being, and that what is " revealed " concerning God in the Bible tells us not what God in His own nature is, but only what He desires that we should believe concerning Him. The revelation is only a quasi-revelation. This theory of modified agnosticism is advocated in an apologetic interest, the design of the Lecturer being to cut away the ground from below opponents of revealed truths by demonstrating the incompetency of speculation on such transcendent themes. The human mind can know nothing really about God ; therefore it cannot know that the mysterious doctrines of the faith are false. There is, however, reason to fear that what was meant for defence, is, in effect, a betrayal of the cause of revelation. As Mr. Maurice put it pithily, the refutation of unbelief costs too much, the cost being the revelation in defence of which the refutation was elaborated. For if revelation be *quasi*, what is the value of it? Is it a revelation at all? If the doctrine of Scripture tell us not what God is, but what He would have us believe Him to be, how can we know that He even wishes us so to think? Is not the wish also quasi? Everything on this hypothesis is quasi. We have a quasi revelation of a quasi wish that we should believe certain propositions as quasi truths concerning a Being who in very deed is utterly unknowable. Can we wonder that men should decline to accept this system of quasis and make-believes, and prefer, with Mr. Herbert Spencer, to take up the position: if the absolute cannot be known, then it is incompetent to make any affirmations concerning it, and the only logical position is theological nescience. If, therefore, we are to hold by a revelation at all, and to escape from naturalistic agnosticism, we must believe with all our heart that God can be known truly, though not adequately —known especially on the moral side of His being. This certainly is the faith of the writers of the Bible, and between this and the agnostic creed there seems no tenable standing-ground. It is possible that the resolute maintenance of the knowableness of God, and of that which goes along with it, the essential identity of the Divine nature and human nature, may increase the pressure of difficulties connected with particular doctrines. But it is folly to seek escape from such difficulties by adopting the sceptical tenet that morality is not the same thing for God that it is for men. Yet such is the position taken up by the Bampton Lecturer, in an apologetic interest. There is an absolute morality, we are told, based upon the nature of God; but what that morality is we cannot imagine. But if we cannot know what the morality is, how can we know that there is a morality for God at all? If Divine morality is not identical with human morality in *kind*—of course they cannot be identical in all particulars—to speak of an absolute morality is simply to put together two mutually cancelling words. Unless we can say that love means for God what it means for man, we had better not say that God is love at all; for the statement conveys no intelligible idea. Far from being a revelation, it is not even sense. On the whole, the chief value of Dr. Mansel's well-meant effort is to present to the world a *reductio ad absurdum* of an apologetic method which reduces revelation to mystery, and relies on a system of external evidences which give no aid to faith or rest to the heart, but at most avail to shut the mouths of gainsayers.

The Bible, then, is indeed profitable for doctrine. The benefit, however, is not to be attained without pains on the learner's part. For the Bible does not supply us with a ready-made summary of the doctrinal import of revelation, stating in so many propositions what knowledge the self-manifestation of God in grace conveys concerning God Himself, concerning man the recipient of His grace, and concerning the blessings which by His grace God confers on man. This propositional or scholastic way of teaching is not at all the manner of the Bible. Nowhere in the sacred

book do we find in tabulated form a statement even
of the more essential truths of revelation, not to
speak of the more detailed doctrines of the second
order of importance which have been extracted from
the Scriptures by the learned investigations of theologians. We do find there an exact summary of
duty; but there is no table of credenda answering to
the table of moral laws given in the Decalogue, setting forth, *e.g.*, that the God of revelation is a Trinity
in Unity; that man is a being made in God's image,
but fallen from the ideal of his nature through sin,
and so depraved that without Divine aid he cannot
fulfil the end of his being; that the benefits which
God in His grace confers on sinful man are the free
pardon of sin and the renewal of his moral nature;
and that the former is conferred for the sake of Jesus
Christ, the Son of God, incarnate and crucified, and
the latter communicated through the gift of the Holy
Spirit as the immanent source of sanctification. In
view of the innumerable controversies that have
arisen in the course of the Christian ages as to what
is to be believed, and the melancholy effect which
these controversies have had in disrupting the Church
into a thousand fragments, it may seem a matter for
wonder and regret that it did not please God to give
in the sacred book a distinct, clear statement of all
that was necessary to be believed in order to salvation, and as a basis for the fellowship of saints—a
sum of saving knowledge not to be subtracted from
or added to. But it may be questioned whether it
were possible to frame a sum of doctrine expressed in
language that should exclude the possibility of doubt
or dispute as to its meaning, on the part even of the

stupid, the subtle, or the perverse.   In any case, such a doctrinal summary has not been vouchsafed.   The Bible conveys to us its didactic lesson in a very occasional, indirect, and indefinite way.   Its method is literary, not dogmatic. It teaches, as it were, without intending to teach ; relates a history, and leaves us to infer the lesson ; indites a psalm expressive of the sentiments awakened in the writer's mind by contemplation of the manifestation which God has made of Himself, and leaves us to find out by poetic sympathy the thought embodied.   The Bible contains all sorts of literature—histories, prophecies, poems lyric and dramatic, proverbs, parables, epistles.   All are profitable for doctrine, but none are dogmatic ; all are excellent for religious edification, but disappointing from the point of view of scholastic theology.   Not even the epistles of Paul can properly be characterised as dogmatic in the scholastic sense.   The four great epistles are full of doctrine of the most important character, but it is conveyed in an occasional, abrupt, vehement way, by a man engaged in a great controversy as to the meaning of Christianity,—whose bosom is agitated by strong emotion, and whose language is a faithful reflection of his feelings—eloquent, but inexact ; crowded with deep, grand thoughts, but with thoughts that struggle for utterance, and are sometimes only half uttered in broken sentences in which grammar is shipwrecked on the rock of heroic passion.   The writing is noble, Divine, inspired in every sense of the term, most profitable for doctrine ; but how different from the style of dogmatic theology, with its careful definitions, and minute distinctions, and cold, passionless, scientific diction !

This account of the Bible, if it do not, as some think, prove that it is neither fitted nor intended to teach doctrine, may, at least, seem to justify despair as to the possibility of extracting from it the due doctrinal use. This, however, is an exaggerated view of the difficulty of using the Scriptures for doctrinal purposes. What has been said as to the style and manner of the sacred writings does not necessarily signify more than this—that to use these writings for such purposes is a delicate task, demanding for its right performance much pains, patience, and wisdom. This is certainly true, and cannot be sufficiently laid to heart. The Bible is a precious gift of God to man, containing the record, the interpretation, and the literary reflection of the revelation of His grace in history. But it is a gift which imposes on those who receive it in faith a heavy responsibility. It does not tell us in a prepared form of words, the didactic significance of its own contents. It leaves us to ascertain that for ourselves. And it is our duty to address ourselves to the task with all diligence and earnestness; for what nobler or more urgent work can we engage in than that of mastering the thought of so unique a volume? But we must enter upon this study with profound humility, mindful how much has been left to ourselves, and mindful also of the risk we are exposed to of performing our part not wisely, but foolishly. We may miss the meaning altogether, and read into the book our errors instead of taking out of it God's truth. We may stop short before we have ascertained even the most essential truths of faith, or we may carry the work of formulating Scripture teaching to excessive lengths, to the effect of compromising the dignity of the sacred book, and weakening in men's minds the reverent esteem in which it ought to be held. The risk of miscarriage somehow is so great that we do well to read with the prayer in our heart—"Send forth Thy light and Thy truth." The actual miscarriage in past ages has been so vast and so disastrous that we may not take amiss the rebuke and scorn of the world. When Shimei cursed David, a fugitive from his throne, the object of malediction, conscious of his own shortcoming, said: "Let him curse, for the Lord hath bidden him." In like manner, when the apostle of modern culture tells professional theologians that they are incompetent, bungling interpreters of Scripture, and that literary men, acquainted with the best products of genius in all languages, are far fitter for the delicate task than they, it becomes those to whom the reproach is addressed to submit to it in silence, sensible of the wrong that has been done to the Divine word by its professional expounders.

In making these observations I do not mean to suggest that Mr. Arnold, or any man of like gifts and spirit, is entitled to sit in judgment on theologians by profession. While readily acknowledging that divines have come grievously short in their endeavours to gather the main sense of Scripture, and that their profession exposes them to certain biassing and blinding influences, I cannot regard the discursive reading of a litterateur as the fittest possible preparation for the interpretation of the sacred writings. If the organ of insight into the Bible be not theological lore, still less is it mere literary taste. The true qualification for the sound understanding of the Divine book is an enlightened Christian consciousness, a mind believing in

redemption, and persuasively influenced by that faith.
No man can even begin to understand the Bible who
does not believe in God's grace, and to whose vocab-
ulary the very word is a stranger. And our insight
into the meaning of holy writ will be in proportion to
the strength of our faith in Divine grace, and the
measure in which it has proved in our experience an
emancipating power, bringing liberty to our reason,
our conscience, and our heart. While grace is not believed in, or while it is believed in feebly, there is a
veil on the face which hides the glory of the Lord as
reflected from the sacred page. To understand the
Scriptures is above all things to understand the lov-
ing-kindness of the Lord; and it may be taken for
granted that he who has narrow thoughts of God's
love, and of the purposes of that love towards mankind, no matter what the extent of his learning may
be, has but a very dim apprehension of the drift of
the Scriptures. And as a mind in which the love of
God has been shed abroad by the Holy Ghost is the
aptest to discern the scope of the Scriptures as a whole,
so is it best able to determine what amid all that is
taught there are the things of chief concern. It dis-
cerns, as if by instinct, what doctrines are most intimately connected with the great central truth of the
purpose of grace. The scholastic dogmatist can determine by proof-texts that this or that dogma is *de
facto* taught in Scripture; but the doctrines are all
alike to him—that they are scriptural is the one consideration in his eyes. But the Christian mind can
determine with some degree of probability which of
all the doctrines that Biblical theology, by its learned
appliances, can extract from the Bible, are of vital im-

portance to faith and life. While accepting all Scripture as profitable for doctrine, it finds in certain teachings of Scripture the food of its life. It can classify doctrines according to their value, and its principle of classification is relationship to the central truth of God's grace. The nearer to that the more vital.

The dogmatic spirit may be jealous of this power of discernment ascribed to the believing mind, and may even see in the claim advanced on its behalf an attempt to set the " inner light " above the written word. This, however, would be a crass misunderstanding. It is one thing to make the Christian consciousness judge of the *truth* of Scripture teaching, quite another to make it judge of its comparative *value*. Surely it is not presumptuous to claim for faith the power to discern that the doctrine of the incarnation is of more importance than a doctrine, based on texts, concerning the exact constitution of Christ's person ; or that the fact that Christ died for our sins is of more moment than any theory of atonement, claiming for itself Scripture support? Not only may the Christian mind distinguish between doctrines at once as to certainty, and as to importance, but it must. The healthy life, both of the individual believer, and of the Church, depends on such distinctions being made, and made wisely. What injury, is it asked, can neglect to classify doctrines as to their importance, occasion? The individual Christian in his indiscriminate zeal for doctrines, for the specialties of his own creed, as distinct from the catholic verities held by all believers, may forget to his loss that the kingdom of God is not meat or drink, or say Calvinism or Arminianism, but righteousness and peace and joy in the Holy Ghost. The Church, through the same zeal, may be unnecessarily divided into mutually exclusive sections, as it is this day to the astonishment of the world and the grief of all Christ-like men. In their attempts at classification of truths in the order of importance, Christians, whether acting individually or collectively may, probably will, err. But that does not excuse neglect of the task. The work has to be done, and it has not been done to our hand, and greater evil may result from leaving it unattempted, than from doing it in a way that falls far short of perfect wisdom.

To draw up an exhaustive list of the great fundamental truths which, like planets, revolve around the Sun of a revelation of grace in the firmament of Scripture, is certainly a task from which, apart from the fear of criticism or contradiction, one may very excusably shrink. Yet there are some truths which, without pretending to exhaustiveness, we may with some measure of confidence characterise as of exceptional importance. To such belong the doctrine of God as manifested in the revelation of grace, the doctrine which unfolds the nature of the gift of grace, and the doctrine concerning man as God's grace finds him and as that grace exhibits him after it has wrought its full effect upon him. As regards the first, the Church in all ages has confessed that God is manifested in the economy of grace as a Trinity in Unity. This truth, as was to be expected, does not come clearly to light till the epoch of fulfilment. It is from the New Testament that we learn concerning the Father, the Son, and the Holy Ghost.

12*

In the unfolding of the doctrine a place of supreme importance belongs to the great event of the *Incarnation*, itself a truth of cardinal importance, as exhibiting Divine grace in action up to the full measure of gracious possibility. No man knew the Father till the Son came and revealed Him, so the Gnostics read the remarkable text in Matt. xi. 27. It is a true saying, though not in the sense they put on it, which was that the God of the Old Testament was an altogether different God from Him whom Jesus made known. The God of the Old Testament is, as we have seen, a God of grace. Nevertheless, speaking comparatively, no man knew the Father till Jesus declared Him. When Jesus came the Fatherhood of God became once for all a fundamental truth of theology, not merely in virtue of His teaching that truth, though that fact exercised a signal influence in giving currency to the doctrine, but still more by His self-manifestation as the Son of God. He offered Himself to the world as a Divine being who had come to earth to seek the lost. Yet He represented Himself as standing in the relation of Son to God as Father. Hence believers in Him learnt to distinguish in God, Father and Son, and to think of the Divine Being as no abstract unity, but as involving plurality. The Son coming in the flesh became the Exegete of God both as to His nature and as to His mind,—in the one respect, in so far as He made known the existence of relationship in God; in the other, in so far as He dwelt among men, Himself a genuine man, "the Son of Man" full of grace, and showed to them that love was the very centre of God's moral being.

But the revelation of Paternity through Sonship does not exhaust the knowledge of God communicated to men by Christ. For He spake to His disciples of a Spirit of truth and purity, Source of illumination and holiness, who should be with them after He had Himself left the world. Of this Spirit He spake as *another*, distinct from His Father and from Himself, yet standing in most intimate relations to both; proceeding from the Father, and in the experience of believers taking the place of Himself, His *alter ego*.* It is true this doctrine of the Spirit occurs chiefly in the representation of Christ's teaching contained in the fourth gospel, which to many in these days is an utterly untrustworthy source of information as to the words actually spoken by our Lord, or at the very least a highly-coloured medium; though, strange to say, Mr. Arnold, for certain reasons, prefers it to the synoptical gospels. But if we are driven from John we can take refuge in Paul. For Paul's acknowledged Epistles contain the same doctrine of God as that which we gather from the four gospels. Paul knows of the grace of the Incarnation, and speaks of it in terms at once explicit and pathetic.† He also knows of a Divine Spirit conceived of not merely as transcendent, source of miraculous charisms, but as *immanent*, dwelling in the Church and in the individual believer as a source of ethical influence, promoting the illumination and sanctification of the body of Christ. This Spirit he calls now the Spirit of God, anon the Spirit of Christ, yea, he sometimes identifies

---

* John xiv. 16.   † 2 Cor. viii. 9.

the immanent Spirit with Christ, saying, the *Lord is the Spirit*,* a view exactly coinciding with that suggested in the fourth gospel, where Jesus in one part of His discourse says: " I will pray the Father and He will give you another Comforter, even the Spirit of truth "; and a little further on: " I will not leave you orphans, I will come to you,"† implying that the other Comforter as a fact of experience will be Christ Himself spiritually present. Are we to look on this doctrine of Paul's concerning Father, Son, and Holy Ghost, and especially concerning the immanent Spirit, as an invention of Paul, the product of his fertile brain working on the original datum that Jesus was the Christ crucified for sin, accepted by him at his conversion? How much more probable that in these letters of his we have a trustworthy reflection of the faith current in the Church some twenty years after the crucifixion, and current because it in turn was a trustworthy reflection of the apostolic tradition concerning the teaching of Christ. That the doctrines of the Incarnation and of the Holy Spirit are not by any means so prominent in the synoptical representation, as in that of the fourth gospel, need be no reason for doubt as to the historicity of the latter. Even inspired men know only in part, and one may know more than another, and a later writer is likely to know more than an earlier as time and events develop the significances of words spoken by Him to whom all bear witness; and therefore it is very credible that the most advanced account of

---

* 2 Cor. iii. 17. See also ver. 18, καθὼς ἀπὸ Κυρίου πνεύματος.

† John xiv. 16, 18.

our Lord's doctrine is not an advance beyond His
words, but towards them and towards a more perfect
comprehension of their meaning,—a development not
beyond, but up to the stature of the great Master.
But suppose it were otherwise, and the doctrine of
Paul and of the author of the fourth gospel concerning
God were developments beyond the letter of Christ's
utterances, due to the action of their minds on the
data of His gospel, what would the position amount
to? Simply to this: that men who believed the
gospel of God's grace found themselves compelled
to think of God as a Trinity; that is to say, that
the doctrine of the Trinity, far from being the idle
speculation that some account it, is simply the form
under which all must think of God who sincerely
believe in a Revelation of Grace. Apart from such
faith that doctrine may appear a mere unintelligible
mystery; to those who believe it may still appear
mysterious, but it will be something more,—darkness
produced by excessive light, grace dazzling by its
brightness.

Of the nature of the gift of grace, of "the things
that are freely given to us of God,"* the Scriptures
contain manifold intimations. Hebrew prophecy
shows us the forms under which the *summum bonum*
presented itself to view in the era of preparation and
hope. The New Testament makes us acquainted
with the aspects under which the same thing was
presented to faith by our Lord and the apostles and
others, authors of New Testament writings. Four
leading types of doctrine on this subject may be

---

* 1 Cor. iii. 12. Τὰ ὑπὸ τοῦ Θεοῦ χαρισθέντα ἡμῖν.

distinguished. The gift of grace is exhibited as the *Kingdom of God*, as the *Righteousness of God*, as *unrestricted Fellowship with God*, and as *Eternal Life*. The first is the keynote or watchword of our Lord's teaching in the synoptical representation, the second is the great theme of Paul's teaching, the third is the leading thought of the Epistle to the Hebrews, and the fourth takes the place of the first in the Johannine account of our Lord's doctrine. It would be an interesting and instructive study which proposed for its aim to develop the significance of each of these respective view-points and their mutual relations. That they are distinct is evident at a glance. The peculiarity of the first is that it exhibits the *summum bonum* as a social thing. The gift of grace, whatever it may be, is not given to men as isolated individuals, but as citizens of a sacred commonwealth. This doctrine is thoroughly congenial to a revelation of grace, for it implies that men cannot be blessed in solitude, but only in and through brotherhood, as sons of God and members of one Divine family. We are therefore not surprised to find that all that Jesus taught concerning the kingdom, bore on its face that the kingdom of God is a kingdom of grace. He said that the kingdom was for the humble, the childlike, the poor, the publicans and sinners, for all who only repented and believed. How could he say more emphatically that the kingdom was a kingdom of grace, a society over which God ruled as a gracious Father, and whose members, whatever their previous characters may have been, were all dear to Him as sons?

Paul's view of the gift of grace is thoroughly distinc-

tive. Jesus had said : " Seek ye the kingdom of God
and His righteousness." The two things named were
the highest goods of life in the esteem of all devout
Israelites. They desired the kingdom, and they
sought after righteousness. Paul sought after both,
and he speaks of both in his writings ; but whereas
Jesus, also speaking of both, yet spake chiefly of the
kingdom, Paul, on the other hand, spake chiefly of
the righteousness of God. The righteousness of God
is the great theme of his principal epistles. It is a
striking form of words, and does not mean what an
inexperienced reader would almost certainly suppose.
By the righteousness of God, Paul means not the
righteousness which conforms to the Divine standard,
or which God demands, but the righteousness which
God *gives*. It is a synonym for God's free grace, bestowing on men forgiveness, and treating them as
righteous irrespective of sin. It is closely connected
in Paul's system of thought with the death of Christ.
That death Paul regarded as an atonement for sin,
the death of the just for the unjust, of the sinless for
the sinful : therefore, as he tells us in one of his epistles, it was a standing part of the gospel which he
preached in every place, that Christ died for our sins.
His doctrine concerning man's relation to God was
that, because of Christ's death, the believing man is
in God's sight as one who never sinned : righteous, a
son, accepted in the *Beloved.* A believing man so
treated by God in His grace, is a man in possession
of the righteousness of God. This doctrine appears
at first not only distinct from that of Christ, but foreign and uncongenial. Yet there is more affinity between it and the doctrine of the Master than appears

on the surface. That God pardons men for Christ's sake is a doctrine identical with that which Jesus Himself taught when He said, "This is My blood of the New Testament, which is shed for many for the remission of sins."* That pardon and acceptance for Christ's sake should be called the righteousness of God, may seem an artificial mode of speaking, but that is a question of words: the thing so named is acceptable and in harmony with the teaching of Christ. At another point the Pauline doctrine seems to recede from that of Christ, in this respect, viz., that in Paul's system the *summum bonum* seems to be an affair of the individual; while in Christ's teaching, as we saw, it is a social thing. But here, also, the two systems approach each other more closely than is apparent on the surface. For in Paul's view the believer does not obtain the blessing of righteousness in a state of isolation, but as a member of a spiritual organism of which Christ is the head, and Christians the body. This solidarity of believing men with one another and with Christ is the basis of Paul's doctrine of objective or "imputed" righteousness, and that which redeems it from the charge of artificiality, or the still more serious charge of questionable morality.

In the Epistle to the Hebrews, the supreme boon of Divine grace appears as unrestricted absolutely free communion with God. It is set forth as the very mark or distinctive characteristic of the era of the *better hope*, that under it we can draw nigh to God,† with true heart, in full assurance of faith.‡ Christianity is the religion of access, as distinct from the Levi-

---

* Matt. xxvi. 26. † Heb. vii. 19. ‡ Heb. x. 21.

tical religion, which was one of distant relationship : God's honour carefully guarded ; man standing afar off worshipping in awe. There is now no veil within which none may enter except the priests, no second veil beyond which none may penetrate save the high priest, and he only once a year, and not without careful precautions against the consequences of an approach not according to rule. The veils are rent asunder, and the distinction between a holy place and an inaccessible most holy place is annulled. Christians may come into the very presence of God, and have the freedom of all the chambers of the heavenly temple, their Father's house on high. Thither Christ has entered as the great High Priest of humanity, but entered in an entirely new capacity ; not as mere representative or substitute, as in the case of the Aaronic high priest, but as *forerunner.** Aaron went into the most holy place in the people's stead, going into a place where they might not follow him. Jesus, our Priest after the honourable order of Melchisedec, enters the heavenly most holy place as our pioneer, to prepare a place for us as He said to His disciples. This forerunnership of Christ is the originality of Christianity as compared with the Levitical religion, and it is its glory. It is the conclusive proof of its being the perfect and therefore the eternal religion. A religion which kept men standing at a distance

---

* Heb. vi. 20, unhappily translated in the English version " whither the forerunner is for us entered, even Jesus"; as if the idea of forerunner were one familiar to the Hebrews, whereas it was a novelty, and as such is introduced here. The passage should be rendered—" Whither *as* forerunner is for us entered Jesus."

awe-stricken, and hedged God about with mystery to guard His majesty from violation, could not be the final form of the relation between God and man. The existence of the veil was an infallible sign of a rude religion, fit only for the childhood of humanity, and but a shadow of good things to come. Such a religion is doomed to be outgrown, antiquated, and superseded. But a religion which abolishes all envious restrictions, and brings man into the most intimate fellowship with God, can never be replaced by a better. It is the best possible, and therefore ought to be perennial ; the perfect, and therefore the final form of man's relation to God. Accordingly, this epistle, in the most emphatic manner, claims for Christianity the honour of being the *eternal religion* in contrast to the Levitical religion, whose transiency is asserted with equal emphasis. That Christianity is the eternal religion is, indeed, the chief thought of the epistle regarded from the apologetic point of view, as the conception of the essence of religion as unrestricted access to God is the leading dogmatic thought.

The great theme of John's gospel, finally, is eternal *life*. This life, as John represents it, is not a future good to be attained after death. It is the true life of man possessed now by every one who knows the true God and Jesus Christ His Son. It is a life independent of time and chance, consisting in blessed fellowship with God through faith and love. But just because the author of the fourth gospel believes in this eternal life, he also believes in the life everlasting. Over one who possesses eternal life death can have no power ; even his body is proof against the law of corruption. All who love God are like God Himself, everlasting. The world passeth away; but he who doeth the will of God abideth for ever. Similar is the doctrine taught by Paul, and, indeed, throughout the New Testament. The conception of eternal life is, in no case, purely *eschatological.* That life is viewed as immanent in the Christian from the moment he becomes a believer. But its nature is conceived to be such that immortality is involved as a corollary. Hence, just because the gospel has brought to light this true life of faith and fellowship with God the fountain of life, it has also brought to light immortality.

The Bible doctrine concerning *man* is at once humbling and inspiring. The grace of God is represented as finding men in a state of serious moral corruption and consequent unblessedness. That this should be so is implied in the very fact of a revelation of grace. They that be whole need not a physician; if, therefore, God has undertaken in behalf of mankind the healer's task, it may be inferred that the patient labours under a grave malady. A variety of significant and pathetic words and phrases are employed to describe man's condition, some very sombre, others more hopeful. The objects of God's gracious compassion are described as sick, lost, blind, asleep, dead, far-off, without strength, subject to vanity. Such terms, on the most moderate interpretation, studious to avoid all theological exaggeration, justify a strong assertion of human guilt, depravity, and wretchedness. The contemplation of such a forlorn plight naturally suggests questions as to its origin. The Bible contains important hints on that subject, which cannot be overlooked by Biblical or dogmatic theology, but which are not so essential to the doctrine of faith as those that describe man's actual condition. The supremely important fact is that sin is here, not how it originated. It was the fact of sin that made a revelation of grace necessary, and it is that fact above all things which we, the beneficiaries of God's grace, need to lay to heart. No man can be a true believer in a revelation of grace who does not lay the fact to heart ; the same thing cannot be affirmed concerning one who is perplexed by the problem of the origin of sin. Even if the Scriptures had contained no intimations on that subject, the need for a Divine interposition in man's behalf would have remained the same, making the same demands on our faith and gratitude.

In proportion as the Bible humbles men by its picture of his natural condition, it exalts him by the prospect it holds out before him. The two parts of its doctrine of man must be looked at together to be justly appreciated. The Bible takes a sombre view of the reality of human character because it has a high ideal of man's nature and destiny. It would not humble him so low if it did not mean to exalt him so high. The exaltation abundantly compensates for the humiliation. Man, as the recipient of Divine grace, is the son and heir of God ; all things are his now and for ever. Being justified by faith, he has peace with God, and rejoices in the hope of the glory of God. Not only so, he rejoices also in tribulations, because they contribute to the development of his character, and therefore to the confirmation of his hope. Not only so, he rejoices above all in God Himself, as his chief good, the bliss of heaven, the Comforter amid present afflictions, by His benignant providence making all things work together for good. These are great benefits, but they do not exhaust the privileges of the justified. Christians have the further honour to be fellow-workers with God in the grand problem of the transformation of the world into the kingdom of heaven. They are a chosen generation, and they have been chosen that they may show forth the virtues of Him who called them out of darkness into light, letting their light shine before men so that men, seeing their good works, may glorify their Father in heaven. They are the salt of the earth, the light of the world, the leaven in the dough.

These, then, are among the more essential truths of the revelation of grace. God manifested as a Trinity through the Incarnation of Christ, and the mission of the Comforter. Men found by God lost, impotent, dead, alienated,—lifted up by His grace into a region of holiness and blessedness; forgiven for the sake of Him who was crucified for sin; admitted to intimate fellowship with God, and made partakers of eternal life; united into a holy commonwealth, in which they are related to God as sons, to each other as brethren, exhibiting in their mutual converse the communion of saints, and, as a spiritual society, having for their high vocation to bring about the consummation of the desires which Jesus taught His disciples to cherish for the advancement of God's glory, the coming of His kingdom ever more extensively, and the doing of His will on earth as it is done in heaven.

It is a short creed; yet he who sincerely owns these truths is a true Christian, accepted of God, a member of the kingdom of God, and worthy to have part in the fellowship of saints; in the best catholic sense of the word, an orthodox believer. Hitherto the fellowship of saints has been broken up and largely nullified by sectional creeds, in which the doctrine of faith is mixed up with the theology of the schools. Perhaps this was inevitable, but it may fairly be questioned if it ever was legitimate, or anything but a calamity due to human infirmity and sin. In any case, the present condition of the world and of the Church forces upon thoughtful men, earnestly concerned for the realization of the Divine ideal, the question whether the past state of things ought to be perpetuated. The Church is enfeebled by divisions and controversies which render the communion of saints little more than a name, and reduces her spiritual influence to a minimum; Christianity, in consequence, seems to have lost its self-propagating power, and to have become a spent force, destined no longer to give rise to important developments. Utter unbelief, originating from scientific, philosophic, or social causes, judging from all observable symptoms, seems to be spreading on every side. Can nothing be done to remedy this state of matters? Must we continue as we are, each sect holding fast by its peculiar dogmas, and all the sects regarding each other with a suspicious eye, and trust to the millennium for the cure of all present evil? Or shall we go to the opposite extreme, and, to accommodate the sceptical spirit of the age, discard all dogmas and doctrines alike, and reduce Christianity to the Deistic Trinity, God, duty, and immortality, as the only religious certainties? Both views have their advocates in the religious world, but it is not likely that deliverance will come from either of these quarters. The hope of the future seems to lie neither in a creedless Church nor in a Church clinging superstitiously to all traditional dogmas, but in a Church which has the will and the wisdom to distinguish between the essential and the non-essential in religious belief, between catholic Christian certainties and matters of doubtful disputation ; in other words, between *doctrines of faith* and *theological dogmas.* The emphasis with which this distinction is insisted on is the index of the value which the Church sets on faith as distinct from opinion ; and that again is the measure of spiritual power. A Church which neglects the distinction, or declines it as illegitimate, is a Nebuchadnezzar's image, compounded of gold, silver, brass, iron, and clay, and possessing the strength only of the weakest part ; or it may be likened to a child, to whom a penny seems as valuable as a shilling or a sovereign—a sure mark of imbecility. It is certainly no part of true wisdom to despise pence, but, on the other hand, it is to be remembered that there is a penny-wisdom which imports pound-folly. The tithing of mint, anise, and cummin may be attended to with such scrupulous care that justice, mercy, and faith are forgotten.

The distinction between doctrines of faith and dogmas of theology is one which should come into play in all departments of the Church's work ; in the preaching of the word, in the conduct of missions, in the construction of confessional documents, and still more in the catechetical instruction of the young. In these days the question is sometimes asked whether preaching should be doctrinal or not. Opinion and practice differ on the point. In the judgment of some the less doctrine, the less definite religious belief, the better the sermon. The taste of others is for sermons saturated with a theological system and expressing all truth in terms of the system. Edification is best promoted by the preacher who avoids both extremes. Sermons should be doctrinal, but not theological; the truths of faith should underlie, and even form the staple of all preaching, but these truths ought to be set forth in simple, untechnical terms. Among the wise counsels in the Directory for Public Worship, prepared by the Westminster Assembly, is one to the preacher not to trouble the minds of his hearers with "obscure terms of art."

It is hardly necessary to point out what an important qualification for success in missionary enterprise it must be to be able to distinguish between the essential and the non-essential in belief, in teaching heathens the elements of the Christian religion. Above all men a missionary ought not to be a theological pedant. This, however, is a mere commonplace, not needing to be insisted on. It is when we proceed to assert the applicability of the distinction now in view to the construction of creeds and catechisms that we are most likely to encounter gainsaying. We are so accustomed to separatism in religion, or to what may be called the club-theory of church-fellowship, that it seems to us almost axiomatic that a creed should embrace all the theological propositions to which we attach importance. Yet nothing is more certain than that if the visible Church ought to exhibit, in the widest sense possible, the fellowship of saints, such fulness is neither possible nor desirable. The more catholic the communion, the less comprehensive the creed. If we aim at catholicity in Church fellowship we must be content with a creed embracing only the essential truths of faith to which enlightened Christian fidelity requires us to bear witness. This principle, thoroughly carried out, would involve considerable retrenchments in all the Reformed confessions.

Catechisms, being intended for the religious instruction of the young, ought to contain only the sincere milk of the word, expressed, as far as possible, in Scriptural terms. In the catechisms of the seventeenth century, milk is mixed with strong meat, doctrine with dogma, Scripture language with the terminology of the schools. The milk is, that God gave Christ to be a Redeemer of sinners, and the Scriptural way of stating the truth would have been to say, "God so loved the world, that He gave His only-begotten Son, that whosoever believeth in Him should not perish, but have everlasting life." But the catechism offers the child strong meat instead of milk, by stating the truth in terms of the dogma of election. Again, the milk is, that Christ exercised the office of a priest by dying on the cross for our sins; the strong meat mixed therewith is the dogma of satisfaction. The aim of a catechism so constructed is to make the catechumens not only believers, but dogmatically orthodox. The result, in a time like the present, is apt to be recoil from the orthodoxy, and, along with that, apostasy from the faith.

In making these observations I am not to be understood as hinting that immediate attempts at recon-

13

struction of creeds and recasting of catechisms are either likely or desirable. No one indeed would desire that such work should be taken in hand till the scope of the distinction between doctrine and dogma is fully realized, and the distinction itself, in all its breadth, frankly accepted. But though the work may be long deferred, there is no reason why one should not freely express his thoughts on the subject, and leave them to work as a leaven in men's minds. In all probability the Church has many long ages before it, and one may devoutly dream of the glory that is to accrue unto God therein as these ages roll on, and muse on the conditions under which that glory is to be advanced. Among these, in the judgment of many earnest men, reconstruction of the Church on a new, wide basis, must take its place. To this opinion I humbly subscribe. The Church is now weak, and among the causes of her weakness are *doubt, division*, and *dogmatism*. To renew her youth, and make a fresh start in a career of victory, she needs *certainty, concord*, and a *simplified creed*.

www.ingramcontent.com/pod-product-compliance
Lightning Source LLC
Chambersburg PA
CBHW021056030726
47496CB00006B/1865